P9-BYY-456

DATE DUE

DEMCO 38-297

The Land and People of

KENYA

PORTRAITS OF THE NATIONS

The Land and People of®

KENYA

by *Michael Maren*

HarperCollins*Publishers*

For Peter Munene Mburu
and
the students and teachers
of the Ngeru Secondary School

Country maps by Robert Romagnoli.

Every effort has been made to locate the copyright holders
of all copyrighted photographs and to secure the necessary
permission to reproduce them. In the event of any questions arising
as to their use, the publisher will be glad to make necessary
changes in future printings and editions.

THE LAND AND PEOPLE OF
is a registered trademark of
HarperCollins Publishers.

The Land and People of Kenya
Copyright © 1989 by Michael Maren
Printed in the U.S.A. All rights reserved.
For information address HarperCollins Children's Books, a division
of HarperCollins Publishers, 10 East 53rd Street, New York, NY 10022.
10   9   8   7   6   5   4   3   2

Library of Congress Cataloging-in-Publication Data
Maren, Michael.
    The land and people of Kenya / by Michael Maren.
        p.   cm. — (Portraits of the nations series)
    Bibliography: p.
    Includes index.
    Summary: Introduces the history, geography, people, culture,
government, and economy of Kenya.
    ISBN 0-397-32334-4 : $.—ISBN 0-397-32335-2 (lib. bdg.) :
$
    1. Kenya—Juvenile literature.   [1. Kenya.]   I. Title.
II. Series.
DT433.522.M37   1989   88-22959
916.76′2—dc19   CIP
                                                            AC

Contents

THE WORLD

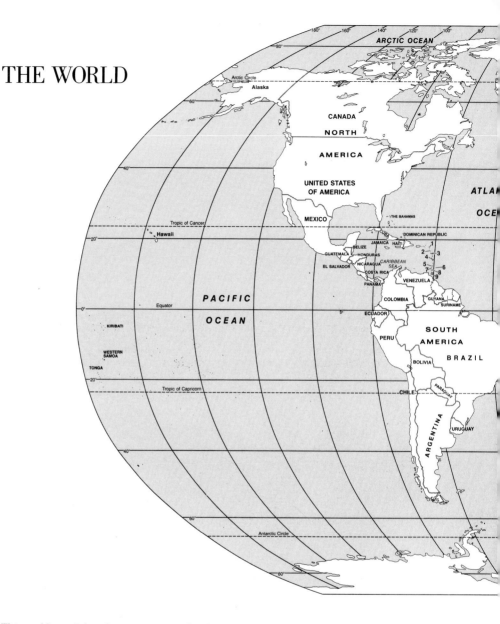

This world map is based on a projection developed by Arthur H. Robinson. The shape of each country and its size, relative to other countries, are more accurately expressed here than in previous maps. The map also gives equal importance to all of the continents, instead of placing North America at the center of the world. *Used by permission of the Foreign Policy Association.*

Legend

——— International boundaries

·········· Disputed or undefined boundaries

Projection: Robinson

| 0 | 1000 | 2000 | 3000 Miles |

| 0 | 1000 | 2000 | 3000 Kilometers |

Caribbean Nations

1. Anguilla
2. St. Christopher and Nevis
3. Antigua and Barbuda
4. Dominica
5. St. Lucia
6. Barbados
7. St. Vincent
8. Grenada
9. Trinidad and Tobago

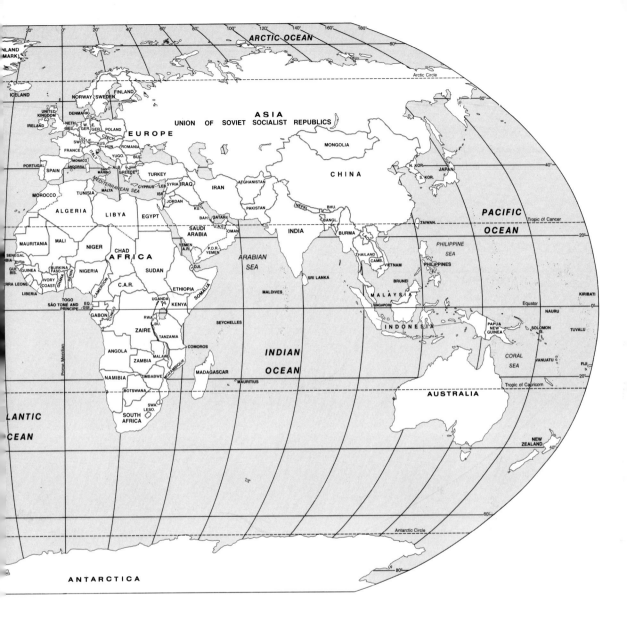

Abbreviations

ALB.	—Albania	C.A.R.	—Central African Republic	LEB.	—Lebanon	RWA. —Rwanda
AUS.	—Austria	CZECH.	—Czechoslovakia	LESO.	—Lesotho	S. KOR. —South Korea
BANGL.	—Bangladesh	DJI.	—Djibouti	LIE.	—Liechtenstein	SWA. —Swaziland
BEL.	—Belgium	E.GER.	—East Germany	LUX.	—Luxemburg	SWITZ. —Switzerland
BHU.	—Bhutan	EQ. GUI.	—Equatorial Guinea	NETH.	—Netherlands	U.A.E. —United Arab Emirates
BU.	—Burundi	GUI. BIS.	—Guinea Bissau	N. KOR.	—North Korea	W. GER. —West Germany
BUL.	—Bulgaria	HUN.	—Hungary	P.D.R.–YEMEN	—People's Democratic	YEMEN A.R.—Yemen Arab Republic
CAMB.	—Cambodia	ISR.	—Israel		Republic of Yemen	YUGO. —Yugoslavia

Mini Facts

OFFICIAL NAME: Republic of Kenya

LOCATION: East Africa, bordering the Indian Ocean on the east, and straddling the equator. To the east is Somalia, to the north Sudan and Ethiopia, to the west Uganda and Lake Victoria; Tanzania is to the south.

AREA: 224,081 square miles (580,367 square kilometers), slightly smaller than Texas.

POPULATION: 22 million (1986 estimated)

CAPITAL: Nairobi

TYPE OF GOVERNMENT: Republic

LANGUAGES: English, Swahili, Kikuyu; other regional languages and dialects

RELIGIONS: Islam, 6%; Catholicism, 16%; Protestantism, 38%; animism and traditional religions, 40%.

HEAD OF STATE (and Head of Government):   President (five-year term)

NATIONAL ASSEMBLY: 158 legislators elected every five years, or sooner if it is dissolved by the president. All candidates are from one party, KANU, the Kenya African National Union.

ADULT LITERACY: 60% (males), 34.8% (females)

LIFE EXPECTANCY: 51.2 years (males), 54.7 (females)

MAIN SOURCES OF FOREIGN EXCHANGE: Exports of coffee, tea, and pyrethrum; tourism

MONETARY UNIT: Shilling

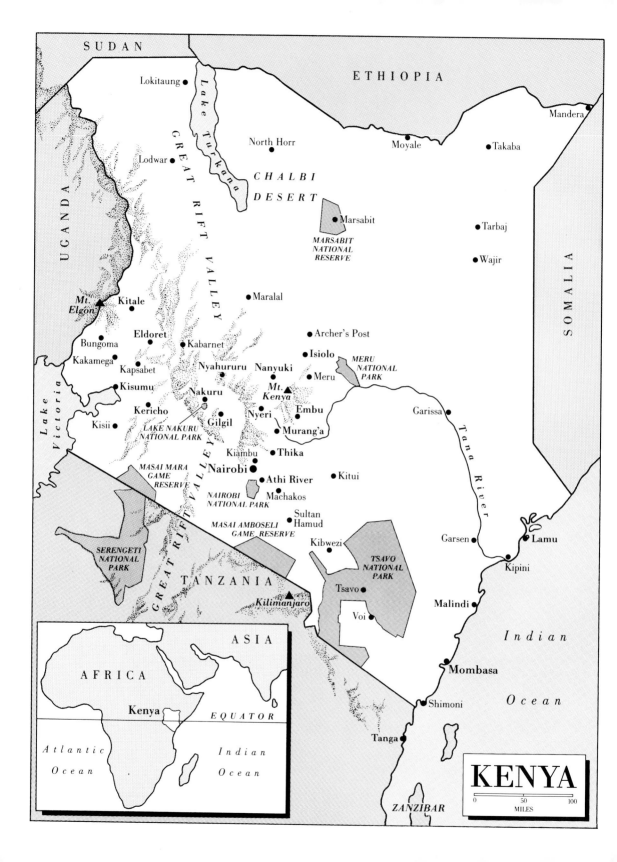

A Morning in Kenya

When the sun rises in central Kenya, the first light strikes the top of Mount Kenya, turning the jagged ice-capped peak into a glowing diamond in the sky. It is six A.M. Because Kenya straddles the equator, there are exactly twelve hours of daylight every day, and because there is no electricity in many villages, each daylight hour is important. Most of the women in the small village on the mountainside have already been up for several hours, relighting yesterday's fires, milking the cows, and preparing the maize-meal porridge that the children will eat before going to school.

It is cold outside, but as soon as the sun burns away the early-morning mist, the air will become hot and dry.

Behind the four mud-and-thatch houses that make up this family's compound is a row of broad-leafed banana plants that bend, nearly touching the thick red-clay soil under the weight of their fruit. Around the bananas the family has planted maize (a white, large-kernel corn) and beans, the staple foods of the region. Nearly every meal will consist of maize, beans, or both.

On the other side of the family compound, in front of the houses, are several rows of coffee trees. The branches are thick with the dark-red berries. Only one more week until the harvest. Then the children will stay home from school to help with picking and transporting the berries to the central market, where officials of the coffee cooperative will purchase them. Here in the highlands of central Kenya, most people manage to earn a good living from their coffee. That is all the money that the family will earn until next season, and they hope that the prices will be good this year.

One hundred miles to the south, in Kenya's vast, open plains, the nomadic Masai people are on the move with their cattle. The young boys, naked, run alongside the herds, their sticks slapping the ground with a cracking sound to keep the cattle from straying too far from the path. The herds kick up huge clouds of billowing dust that can be seen from miles away.

On a nearby hilltop, older boys who are now warriors, or *morani*, walk proudly in a group, their faces stained red with ocher, long silver spears at their sides. They are on the watch for lions or other wild animals that might threaten the herd. During their warrior years the young men are not required to work with the cattle. They are to learn to fight and to survive.

In northeastern Kenya a Somali boy is leading four camels across the sand to a well seeking water. He holds the lead camel, and the other three are tied in a line behind them. He carries in his hand a flat board called a *lak*. Written on the board in Arabic is a section of the Koran, the Moslem holy book, that he is to memorize. When he is finished memorizing that section, his teacher will erase it and inscribe another section for him to study.

In western Kenya, Luo fishermen sit on the shores of Lake Victoria untangling their nets and preparing to spend another day fishing in their small wooden boats. Not far away the eyes of a crocodile peer silently across the surface of the lake.

In the fertile marshlands around the lake, stalks of sugarcane arc high over the heads of women who have come to begin the harvest. Each woman carries a machete, called a *panga* in Swahili. The cane is felled with a single swipe of the razor-sharp blade, and the women will then

A fisherman on Kenya's coast prepares his nets.   J. C. Carton / Bruce Coleman Inc.

carry bundles of the stalks to waiting trucks. Sometimes they will stop work to slice off a small piece of the cane. They bite into the fibrous core of the cane, extracting its sweet juice. Young children on their way to school pass by the fields, and the women pass along some small pieces of cane as an early-morning treat.

In Nairobi, the capital, young men position themselves at intersections, preparing to sell the morning newspapers to drivers when the morning rush hour begins. Kenya has three daily newspapers in English and one in Swahili. They also sell *Time* and *Newsweek.*

Throughout the city and in small towns and villages people are preparing *chai*, or tea the way Kenyans like it, sweet and milky. Men and women are beginning to gather in *chai* houses to relax before going to work in the fields or in factories or banks or government offices.

Outside of Nairobi long lines of workers, men and women, begin their trek into the city's industrial center. They are poorly paid, and even the few cents that it costs to take the bus are more than most workers can afford. So they walk, some of them up to ten miles each way to work.

At Kenya Breweries on the outskirts of Nairobi trucks loaded with Kenyan beer roar to life, diesel engines coughing clouds of black smoke. They will bring the popular Tusker, White Cap, and Pilsner beers to restaurants and bars across the country. The brewery is Kenya's largest industry.

In the flat wastes of the savanna wood-carvers from the Kamba ethnic group set up shop under a baobab tree and begin to chisel away at heavy black ebony. Each cut of the chisel is compact and economical, and in minutes the images of giraffe and impala take shape.

Across the country, even in the most remote villages, people tune their radios to the Voice of Kenya, which broadcasts the national anthem and the morning news in Swahili and English, the national languages. The men sitting in the tea houses listen carefully and speak to each other in their native languages: Kikuyu, Somali, Masai, Luo, or any of forty more languages that are spoken in Kenya.

The news tells them that President Daniel arap Moi will be visiting some towns in western Kenya, where he will be opening a new road and a new school that local people have built with their own money.

At Nairobi's Kenyatta International Airport a Kenya Airways jumbo jet lands with tourists from Europe, America, and Japan. Tourism is one of Kenya's main industries; many people come to visit game parks to see the wildlife for which Kenya is so well known.

People emerge from a Nairobi nightclub and squint in the bright sunlight. The band is still playing inside, but they go across the street for breakfast: *chai* and *maandazi*, a sweet fried bread. In the streets of Nairobi vendors are awaiting the tourists' arrival by lining up carvings and jewelry that they will sell as souvenirs. They also sell baskets made of sisal that have become popular around the world as "Kenya baskets." The baskets are hand dyed, and are woven by women who do the work whenever their hands are free—while walking around or while riding in a bus.

Near the Hilton Hotel, caravans of minibuses are lined up and waiting to transport a group of American tourists to the famous Masai Mara Game Park. They will drive across the plains, see the herds of elephants, and sit in their cars as lions inspect the tires. Then they go to one of the park's tourist lodges, have dinner, relax, and tell of their daily adventures.

At the Nairobi railway station, trains are being loaded with sacks of coffee bound for the port of Mombasa, from where it will be exported to Europe and the United States. Passengers arrive in Nairobi after taking the overnight train from the coast. The trip is a step back in time. The old train moves slowly along the rails, but passengers enjoy some old-style service and luxury.

In great outdoor markets across the country women are laying out blankets or tables with cabbages, tomatoes, carrots, and a green leafy vegetable the Kenyans call *sukuma wiki.* The term means "push the week" in Swahili, and it is what people eat toward the end of the week when they don't have much money.

In Nairobi children in neat school uniforms, like those that are worn in England, are being driven to school by their parents while others wait for the city buses. In the countryside young children in tattered uniforms run barefoot over village paths, heading toward primary schools that are often just mud buildings. There they will sit on the floor or on crude benches for their studies. Though they are the children of poor farmers or herders, they will be expected to learn to speak English by the time they are finished with primary school. If they don't, they won't be allowed to continue on to secondary school, where everything is taught in English.

And if a student can get through secondary school and pass all the exams, he or she just might be able to go on to the University of Nairobi, where the best students from across the country come to study. Their fees and expenses are paid by the government.

In the central part of the city people board *matatus,* small private buses that branch out from there to all points in the country. The *matatus* have no schedules. They leave only when full, so the drivers plead with customers, trying to convince them that they will be the next to leave. They honk their horns and shout, creating a constant din that no one seems to mind. People crowd into the *matatus* carrying huge sacks of vegetables, little children, and perhaps a goat or a chicken.

The market at Limuru, near Nairobi. Piles of maize and beans, Kenyans' staple foods, and other vegetables are sold by farmers in the markets to earn extra cash. It is almost always the women who do the buying and selling in Kenya. Y. Lermann / United Nations

Masai warriors covered with beads and carrying spears walk down the main streets, weaving between parked cars as they might walk through herds of cattle. At an outdoor café, two Kenyan businessmen wearing suits and ties are making a deal with a Japanese man. At the next table an old British gentleman checks football (soccer) scores from England in Kenya's *The Daily Nation.* A chanting call to prayer emanates from

A matatu *stage in Meru Town, northeast of Mount Kenya. These privately owned taxis provide for most of Kenya's transport needs, bringing goods and people from towns to small villages. They are almost always overcrowded and very dangerous. Despite repeated warnings from the government,* matatu *owners continue to overload their vehicles and ignore safety regulations.*   Michael Maren

Nairobi's central mosque.

Beggars, many crippled or deformed, hold out their hands in search of aid. Young boys with secondary-school educations roam the streets searching for work. Often these youths turn to crime or join gangs in order to survive. They live in a shantytown made of cardboard and scraps of wood and tin. Back in the shantytown a child sits in the dirt near an open sewer and plays with a Coca-Cola bottle, the only toy she has.

Only a few miles from the city center in Nairobi game park, a herd of elephants moves across the plains like a dark-gray wall. Some zebras swat flies with their tails while keeping a wary eye on a pride of lions resting nearby. The zebras feel confident that the lions won't be hungry until evening. In the background is the thirty-four-story Kenyatta Conference Center and the Nairobi skyline.

On the Indian Ocean coast a small boat called a *dhow* sails silently southward carrying a load of coconut oil from the island of Lamu to the city of Mombasa. The Arab traders in the region have sailed boats like these for centuries, trading gold, ivory, spices, and slaves among Arab sultanates. Today the dhows carry tape players as well as the spices of old.

Veiled Swahili women covered entirely in black hurry along the narrow streets of Lamu on their way to the market as some men wearing white robes wash their feet at an outdoor spigot and prepare to enter a mosque. The Kenyan coast has been a melting pot of peoples for centuries. Arabs, Africans, and Indians meshed their customs and developed the Swahili culture and language. The coast is where most of Kenya's Moslems live.

The Somali boy in northern Kenya has just finished watering his camels and has begun studying the Koran when he hears a loud roar in the distance. In another instant four jet planes from the Kenya Air Force roar over his head, leaving white streaks across the sky. Within minutes the planes have crossed into the lush green highlands where some women digging in the coffee *shambas* (a *shamba* is a small family farm) with children strapped to their backs glance upward for a moment. The planes enter and then emerge from the clouds that have now hidden the peak of Mount Kenya. A few minutes later they cut across to the southern side of the mountain, where a Masai warrior raises his spear in salute.

The planes then bank toward the east and quickly climb until they disappear into the bright sun. The only sound on the savanna is that of the wind as it whistles through the thorns of acacia trees.

The Land

An American teacher in Kenya was often asked the same question by his students: "*Mwalimu*, where is your *shamba* in the U.S.?"

"I don't have a *shamba*," he would tell them. "I now live here in Kenya."

"No, no," the students would respond, shaking their heads. "This isn't your home. Your home is where you have your land back in America."

"But I have no land in America. My parents have a home in the suburbs with about an acre or so, but that is no longer my home."

"Only one acre? What can they grow there?"

"Nothing. Only some grass and shrubs."

"Then your father must be a very poor man."

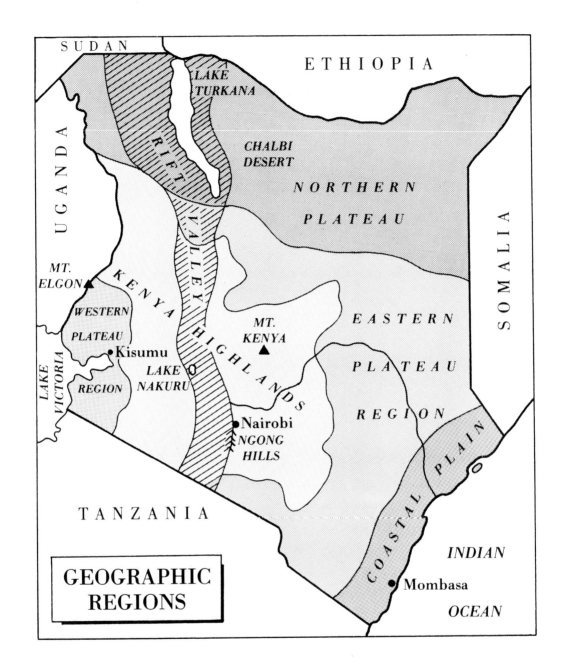

SUDAN

ETHIOPIA

LAKE
TURKANA

CHALBI
DESERT

NORTHERN

PLATEAU

UGANDA

MT.
ELGON ▲

WESTERN

PLATEAU

LAKE
VICTORIA

REGION

Kisumu

LAKE
NAKURU ◯

KENYA

RIFT VALLEY HIGHLANDS

MT.
KENYA ▲

EASTERN

PLATEAU

REGION

SOMALIA

Nairobi
NGONG
HILLS

COASTAL PLAIN

◯

TANZANIA

INDIAN

Mombasa

OCEAN

GEOGRAPHIC
REGIONS

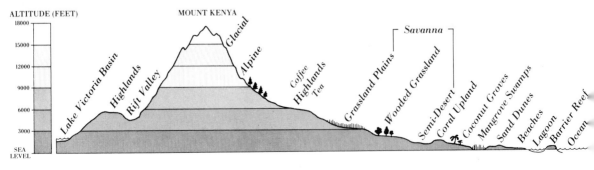

ALTITUDE (FEET)

18000

15000

12000

9000

6000

3000

SEA
LEVEL

MOUNT KENYA

Savanna

Glacial

Alpine

Lake Victoria Basin

Highlands

Rift Valley

Coffee
Highlands
Tea

Grassland Plains

Wooded Grassland

Semi-Desert

Coral Upland

Coconut Groves

Mangrove Swamps

Sand Dunes

Beaches

Lagoon

Barrier Reef

Ocean

"Well, no, he is not."

This fact of American life was incomprehensible to the Kenyan students. No matter how much the teacher protested, they would insist that he must somewhere have a piece of land that was his own, given to him by his father, where he would someday settle to raise his own family.

For in Kenya, every Kenyan man, even if he lives in Nairobi in a large modern house, still considers the plot of land where he was born to be his home. It is where he is from and where he will eventually return. Without land a man has no identity, no roots, no wealth, and nothing to give to his sons. Without land, there is no future.

More than 85 percent of Kenya's people earn their livelihood from the land. Kenyans' attachment to their land has been the driving force behind many aspects of Kenya's history, politics, economics, culture, and religion. Love of land was behind the intense resentment that Africans felt when European settlers came and claimed some of the most fertile land for their own, and it fueled a bloody revolt against British colonialism. Land also plays an important role in modern politics, for there is not enough land in Kenya to support its rapidly growing population. The land shortage and related problems are the most serious challenges that Kenya faces today.

Geography

Kenya is a relatively large country. Its 224,000 square miles (580,000 square kilometers) make it slightly smaller than Texas, or slightly larger than France. Located in East Africa, it is bordered to the southeast by the Indian Ocean, to the south by Tanzania, and to the east by Somalia.

Uganda and Lake Victoria provide the western border, and Sudan and Ethiopia are in the north. Kenya's coast and its western border with

Uganda are natural borders of water and mountains. But the eastern, southern, and northern borders are products of colonial history, straight lines drawn across undifferentiated wilderness by a ruler placed on a map.

With all this land, why is there a land shortage in Kenya? Less than one third of Kenya's land is arable (that is, suitable for agriculture). And only around 15 percent of the country receives adequate rainfall for two dependable growing seasons.

In Kenya's agricultural regions, two rainy seasons assure healthy crops. The short rains fall from October to November. They are called the short rains because they are broken up by periods of sunshine, often in the late afternoon. The long rains, from March through May, are torrential. Day after day the water pours from the blackened skies. The two rainy seasons turn the areas around Lake Victoria, the highlands, and the coast into a rich agricultural resource. Here, tea and coffee are grown for export. Food crops such as maize and beans, as well as sugarcane, coconuts, and cashews at the coast, are grown for local consumption. Seventy-five percent of Kenya's 22 million people live in these areas, where population density can reach 640 people per square mile (400 per square kilometer).

The thing that visitors find most striking about Kenya's land is its awesome beauty, made all the more striking by the varieties of terrain and the diversity of land formations found within the country's various regions. Within Kenya's borders are nearly every type of landscape found on planet Earth.

Kenya can be divided into six distinct geographic regions. Moving generally from east to west across the country they are: The coastal plain, the eastern plateau region, the northern plateau region, the Kenya Highlands, the Rift Valley, and the western plateau region.

Sometimes the changes from region to region are gradual, as is the case between the coast and the savanna. Moving to the northwest from the coast, the land sweeps gently upward, rising to plateaus and grassy plains. Between other regions the contrasts are grand and distinct, marked by vertical escarpments that form massive natural barriers.

The Coastal Plain

Parts of Kenya's coast look like a classic tropical paradise. Long, white sandy beaches bordered with coconut-palm trees provide a welcome to the warm, blue waters of the Indian Ocean. The water is calm because the coast is protected by a coral reef that breaks the incoming waves. The reef is home to an endless variety of sea life, including a diverse and colorful assortment of tropical fish.

The coastline is also spotted with islands that have been used for centuries as ports. The most populous of these islands is the one on which the city of Mombasa is located. With its port of Kilindini, East

Old Town in Mombasa. Mombasa still reflects its Arab, African, Portuguese, Asian, and British pasts.   Africa Report

Africa's busiest, Mombasa is Kenya's second largest city. Goods bound for Uganda, Rwanda, Burundi, Zaire, and southern Sudan are unloaded at the port and taken the rest of the way by road.

The city of Mombasa revolves around the activities of the port. Several navies put down anchor at Mombasa to provide rest and relaxation to their sailors. Mombasa's clubs and bars are often packed with young American, British, French, or Soviet sailors, who enjoy their time on shore. Sailors from merchant ships and tourists on cruises also take advantage of Mombasa's plentiful nightlife and the region's inviting beaches.

Farther up along the coast is the island of Lamu. Lamu is a port for dhows, the Arab sailing ships that have traded along the East African and Arabian Peninsula coasts for hundreds of years. The island looks much as it did centuries ago. There is only one road on the island wide

A weaver on Kenya's coast turns homegrown cotton into cloth. The robes that he is wearing are woven from the same material. The Hutchison Library

enough to drive a car on, and there is only one car there anyway—a Land Rover that is used by the government. People use donkeys for transporting goods from the dhows through Lamu's narrow streets.

The island produces coconut oil and mangrove poles for export. Mangroves are trees that grow in swamps along Kenya's coast. The mangrove poles are used in the construction of the traditional Arab houses of the region. They form the inside support structure that is later covered with a limestone-and-cement mixture.

Today Lamu is a popular tourist destination, as is Malindi, farther south along the coast.

The Eastern Plateau Region

Moving inland from the coast, one sees that the land becomes flat and more barren. This area of rocky soils and scattered thorny scrub brush is called savanna. The savanna is what is usually shown in wildlife films, many of which are shot in Kenya. The rolling plains are crowded with herds of elephants, wildebeests, gazelles, giraffes, and zebras. Flat-topped acacia trees, also called thorn trees, spot the landscape. Water is scarce and seasonal, and the land is sparsely populated.

Though this land produces no commodities for export, it does produce income for Kenya. Here is where most of the tourists go when they come to Kenya on *safari*. They come to see the huge variety of wildlife for which Kenya is famous. Large parts of the savanna have been turned into game reserves where hunting is prohibited and the only shooting is by the tourists with their cameras.

The largest of the reserves, Tsavo, is about the size of the state of Massachusetts. The story of Elsa the lioness, made famous by the book and film *Born Free*, took place in the Meru reserve, northeast of Mount Kenya. In some of the more popular game parks, such as Masai Mara in the Rift Valley on the Tanzanian border, buses packed with tourists

Rivers in northern Kenya rise suddenly in response to rains that fall sometimes hundreds of miles away. The flow of water may last anywhere from a couple of hours to a few months, depending on the season and where the rain is. Palm trees and other plants flourish on the riverbanks, cutting lush pathways through a barren desert. Amy Zuckerman

are as plentiful as the impala that lope across the plains.

One of the main features of the otherwise flat plains are the Taita Hills, which rise to over 6,900 feet (2,100 meters). The Amboseli and Serengeti plains are also in this region. During the wet season part of the Amboseli is covered with the 38-square-mile (100-square-kilometer) Lake Amboseli. But during the dry season the lake disappears, leaving

behind a huge bowl of chalky white dust. Many a tourist has gone looking for Lake Amboseli during the dry season and gone away wondering why so large a lake was so difficult to find.

The western edge of the eastern plateau region borders the Kenya Highlands. And to the north it becomes the northern plateau.

The Northern Plateau

The northern plateau accounts for three fifths of Kenya's territory but is the least populated region of the country. During colonial times the British called it the Northern Frontier District. Much of it was uncharted and only lightly populated.

Like the eastern plateau, much of the northern plateau is covered with scrub brush and acacia trees. Toward the border with Somalia the region is more desertlike. The soil is sandier and the vegetation is sparser. The towns in the eastern part of this region, Wajir and Mandera, are populated predominantly by people of Somali origin.

To the west across the northern plateau is Mount Marsabit, an extinct volcano that rises high above the flatlands below and, therefore, receives more rain and is covered with lush vegetation. The crater of the volcano is now filled with water and is used as a watering hole by elephants and other animals from the plains. The town of Marsabit on the mountain is used as a trading center by many of the nomadic and seminomadic people who live in the region.

This region also holds Kenya's only real desert, the Chalbi. The rivers that traverse the desert and the other arid areas can appear suddenly when rains fall miles away in the mountains, and then, just as suddenly, disappear—leaving behind beds of sand. The force of the onrushing water is so sudden and strong that it has been known to sweep away large trucks that were in the riverbed.

There, when it is dry, elephants can be seen digging in the sand for the water that remains trapped beneath it. The people who live in these areas, too, depend upon the riverbeds for water. Soon after the rains, water can be found just below the surface. But as the dry season goes on, people must dig deeper and deeper to find the water they need.

Farther west is Lake Turkana, which is also the northernmost point of the Rift Valley in Kenya. Looking like a finger pointing into Ethiopia, this 100-mile-long (160-kilometer-long) lake is surrounded by a rocky desert. Though several rivers flow into the lake, there is no outlet, which makes it slightly salty. Like all salt lakes Turkana affords buoyancy for swimmers—but the lake is also home to thousands of crocodiles.

The Turkana people, who live near the lake with their cattle, do not

In northern Kenya a nomad has her entire house on the back of this donkey. It will be set up and covered with grass when she arrives at a suitable spot.   The Hutchison Library

eat fish. For many years the only fishing in the lake was by the small group of El Molo people who lived on an island at the southeastern end of the lake, and they took only a few fish for their own consumption. The remoteness of the lake and the difficulty of transporting goods to and from the region prevented the lake from becoming a commercial fishing center. Today, however, a new road reaches the Turkana region, and fishermen from Lake Victoria have begun setting up operations on the lake. What was only recently one of the world's most isolated regions is now becoming a center of commercial activity.

Turkana is also where Richard Leakey, son of the well-known archaeologists Louis and Mary Leakey, found some of the oldest human remains ever known, supporting the theory that the first humans inhabited the Rift Valley.

From Lake Turkana to the border with Somalia, nomads move with their cattle in a constant search for water and forage. The small towns in the north—Lodwar, Loiyangalani, Isiolo, Maralal, and Marsabit—serve as trading posts and meeting places for the nomads to sell some cattle, camels, milk, or hides in return for cloth, soap, cooking oil, or perhaps a watch or a bottle of Coca-Cola.

Isiolo, the southernmost town in the region, lies at the base of the Kenya Highlands, and is where the nomads from the north meet and trade with the agriculturalists of the south.

Kenya Highlands   Kenya's stark contrasts are best illustrated by the fact that in there is snow on the equator. On a clear day a Somali nomad leading his camel across the northern desert can look up and see the snow-covered peaks of Mount Kenya, an extinct volcano and the central feature of the Kenya Highlands. Looking northward from the slopes of Mount Kenya, one can see a field of smaller extinct volcanoes, giving the area the look of a prehistoric landscape.

Mount Kenya's snow-capped peaks.   The Hutchison Library

The northern slopes of Mount Kenya are broad meadows that are used for growing wheat, while the southern and eastern slopes buckle into thousands of interlocking gorges and ridges that make the area as beautiful as it is difficult to traverse. This is coffee country, where small farmers devote most of the fertile land to this important crop. Towns and villages of Kikuyu, Meru, and Embu people line the tops of the ridges, while coffee trees cover the sides of the terraced hills. The Kikuyu traditionally worshiped the commanding peaks of the mountain, calling it Kere-Nyagah, Mountain of Light. The name Kenya is derived from the name of the mountain.

Mount Kenya

The country of Kenya takes its name from the most prominent geographic feature in the area, Mount Kenya.

In 1849 Johann Ludwig Krapf, a German missionary traveling in East Africa, became the first European to see what is now called Mount Kenya. He described the mountain peak as "two large horns or pillars, as it were, rising over an enormous mountain . . . covered with a white substance," which he took to be snow. As the mountain peak was located almost directly on the equator, the European scientific community declared that Krapf was a crackpot, a liar, or worse. It was only later that science became aware of the effect of altitude on temperature, and that indeed the 17,058-foot (5,199-meter) mountain was topped with snow, as was its cousin to the south, Kilimanjaro. (Temperature drops 3°F [1.7°C] for each 1000 feet [300 meters] of altitude.)

The Kikuyu people, who live near the mountain, pronounced it as *Kere-Nyagah.* When Krapf first saw the mountain, however, he was many miles away, where another ethnic group, the Kamba people, lived. The Kamba speak a language that is very similar to that of the Kikuyu, but they don't pronounce their *r* or *g* sounds. So when Krapf asked what the mountain was called he probably heard something like *"kehenyah,"* which he mispronounced as Kenya. The place soon became known as the Mount Kenya region, then the Mount Kenya Colony, then just the Kenya Colony. Finally, on December 12, 1963, it became the Republic of Kenya, an independent country.

A second extinct volcano, Mount Elgon (14,177 feet, or 4,321 meters) stands on Kenya's border with Uganda at the far-western edge of the Highlands. This is one of the most densely populated rural areas of the world. On the roads and paths that divide the *shambas* in the region, people can be seen walking shoulder to shoulder as if they were in an urban area.

Here the pressure on the land is the greatest. In earlier generations, when land was plentiful, people could take what land they could cultivate. Having many children meant that a family could hold more land and grow more food. But that is no longer true today.

The area is generally cool and dry—what most people consider to be perfect weather. At some points where people live at 10,000 feet (3,000 meters), it actually becomes extremely cold, sometimes reaching freezing temperatures during Kenya's cold season in July.

The Rift Valley

The Rift, which separates eastern from western Kenya, is one of the world's geological wonders. This huge split in the earth runs from southern Turkey to Mozambique in southern Africa. The Red Sea, where Africa splits from the Middle East, is part of the Rift. And its path can be traced through Africa by following the line of lakes through Ethiopia, Kenya, Tanzania, and Mozambique.

The Ngong Hills, made famous in the book and film *Out of Africa*, form part of the the eastern escarpment separating the Rift from the Kenya Highlands. The Nyandarua Mountains, rise to over 13,000 feet (almost 4,000 meters), forming another section of the eastern escarpment. (These mountains are still often referred to as the Aberdares, the name given to them by the explorer Joseph Thomson in honor of Lord Aberdare, head of the Royal Geographic Society in 1882.) At points the floor of the Rift lies nearly 3,000 feet (900 meters) below the land above, and in places the valley widens out to 40 miles (65 kilometers).

Mount Longonot is only one of many extinct volcanoes in Kenya. Located in the Rift Valley not far from Nairobi, it is a popular destination for climbers and tourists who sometimes picnic on its peaks.   The Hutchison Library

At the southern end of the Rift in Kenya are lakes Baringo, Bogoria, and Nakuru, known for the flamingos whose numbers can turn the lakes' surfaces into a fluttery pink blur. Lake Naivasha is a popular resort outside of Nairobi, and Lake Magadi produces soda ash.

At the western edge of the Rift the land once again rises to form several magnificent escarpments: the Mau Escarpment, which rises to over 9,800 feet (3,000 meters), and the Elgeyo Escarpment and Cherangani Hills, over 10,500 feet (3,200 meters) above sea level. Here again the land is high, fertile, and heavily populated.

The Western Plateau Region

From the western escarpments the land slopes downward to form the Lake Victoria Basin.

A steamboat and a sailboat on Lake Victoria. Once an important waterway, Lake Victoria's ports are not used as much as they once were.   East African Railways & Harbours

Victoria is the world's second-largest lake, and was named for the British monarch by the first Europeans to arrive at its shores.

Kenya's third-largest city, Kisumu, sits on the shores of this inland sea. Kisumu was once an important port, connecting the central African interior with the railroad to the port of Mombasa. Today, road transport dominates the interior trade, and much of the port is quiet, though it serves as the capital of Kenya's Nyanza Province.

Other ports, such as Homa Bay, are still used to a degree and are launching points for Luo fishermen. Some of these areas along the lake do not receive adequate rainfall to make them as agriculturally productive as they could be. Several irrigation schemes using lake water have been set up, and others are in the planning stages.

The Frontiers and the Future

Kenya's population distribution contrasts as sharply as the land. As altitude drops, so too does the amount of vegetation and the number of people the land can support. From parts of the fertile, green, and crowded highlands it is possible to look northward upon the arid browns of the wide-open spaces below.

Kenyans are now looking to the frontier for the future. These are the areas that will have to satisfy Kenyans' hunger for land. Several settlements in the drylands have been established by landless people from the central parts of the country. Pioneers in their own country, they have dug wells and built irrigation systems to bring life to the deserts. Some have planted crops and cut roads through the bush using only picks and shovels. It is the Kenyans' love of land that drives them to work in what are often impossible conditions. They know that their future depends on their ability to make these lands productive.

Like Kenya's people, the land is feeling the pressure to change.

The Peoples

Although the Kenyan people are attached to their land, economic pressures and a shortage of land are driving more and more of them to seek work in the cities. Here the pressures of change and modernization are most deeply felt, and urban life has become increasingly typical of life in modern Kenya.

Nowhere is Kenya's ethnic diversity more evident than in the streets of Nairobi.

Nairobi is one of the world's great cosmopolitan cities. It is a commercial center for East Africa and a meeting place for the world. In the streets of Nairobi people of every possible racial and cultural origin can be seen: Africans, Europeans, Arabs, and people from the Indian subcontinent (called "Asians" in Kenya). And all of them are Kenyans.

Of the 22 million people who live in Kenya, those of European, Asian, and Arab origin make up only around 2% of the population, though their impact has been greater than that because of the economic power that these groups have had since colonial times.

The majority African population comes from more than forty different ethnic groups, which in turn can be divided into more than a hundred subethnic groups, each of which has its home in a different part of the country, each with its own language or dialect, and each with its own customs, traditions, systems of government, laws, and religious beliefs.

At the Nairobi railroad station and the central bus depot people come and go from the rural areas. From some parts of the country it can take days to arrive on a bus, or less time on private *matatus*, converted pickup trucks or minibuses that carry fewer people: Luo people from Kisumu. Masai from Narok. Somalis from Wajir. Turkana from Lodwar. Kalenjin from Kitale. Kikuyu from Nyeri. Swahilis and Giriamas from the coast.

They come to do a little business, see families or friends, while Nairobi dwellers board buses heading back to their home areas to attend weddings or funerals, or to visit parents.

As in many cities, neighborhoods develop that house a concentration of one ethnic group or another. In a section called Eastleigh, for example, many Somalis live. There they have built their mosques, and the restaurants and tea shops serve a special style of Somali spiced tea. People from Meru district gather at the Meru *chai* house and speak in their vernacular and share information about friends and relatives back home.

Most of Kenya's Asians live in Nairobi and in other cities and towns, where they predominate in the wholesale trade. African shopkeepers from the rural areas often come to buy from them to get their best prices

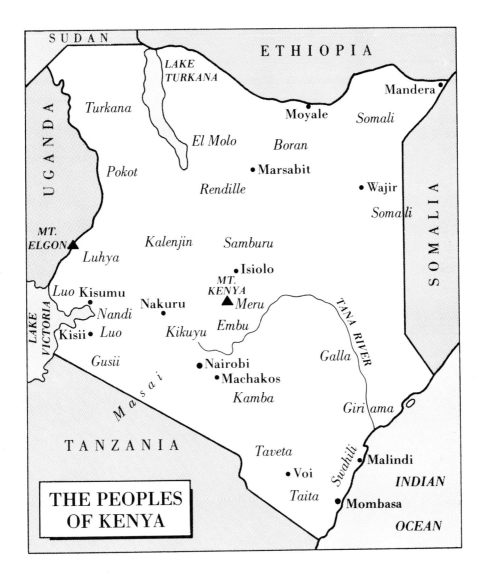

The names of the peoples of Kenya, such as *Samburu*, are printed in italic.
Cities and towns, such as **Nairobi**, are printed in bold.
Placement on this map gives only a rough idea of where each group is centered.

Some Notes on Terminology

The words we use to describe people say much about our attitudes toward them. In the United States people have been sensitive to this. Americans of African descent objected to the old term Negro, left over from the days of slavery, and prefer to be called Black or African-American, which suggest a more positive image.

For the same reason the term ethnic group is used in this book to describe what is often called a tribe. Where tribe suggests small primitive bands, ethnic group more accurately describes a people who have their own language, culture, history, religion, and political system.

Much of the terminology in use concerning Africa expresses the attitudes of European colonists who wanted to believe that the Africans were inferior in order to justify taking African lands and dominating African peoples. Words such as *native* and *boy* were used for this purpose. Other terminology was applied by anthropologists in a misguided effort to prove that Europeans were superior to Africans. Some European anthropologists were disturbed by the fact that the great civilization of Egypt surpassed in education, scholarship, and grandeur any European civilization of the same era. There were also great civiliza-

on canned food, cigarettes, or spare parts for cars and tractors.

Before independence the Asians owned nearly every retail store (or *duka*) in even the smallest villages in Kenya. But at independence, in an attempt to give opportunities to Africans, Asians were told to restrict their activities to the larger towns and cities. Many decided to leave Kenya.

As in most cities, Nairobi also has its neighborhoods that are segre-

tions in Ethiopia. The Europeans refused to believe that anything of value came from Africa. They decided that the Egyptians and other Africans from the north must have been at least part European. So the European anthropologists divided Africans into two groups: Hamites and Negroes. Hamites, they said, included Egyptians and Ethiopians, but also some groups that are found in Kenya, including Somalis and Gallas. The Hamites, they said, were related to Europeans.

But when they arrived in Kenya, the Europeans found a problem with their classification. There they met the Masai, the Samburu, the Boran, and other African ethnic groups who looked more like Ethiopians and Somalis but lived farther south and were culturally more similar to the people the Europeans called Negroes. Scientific logic would have told them that there was something wrong with their classification, but this was politics and racism, not science. Without any proof at all the anthropologists decided that these new groups were the product of the mixing of the Hamites and the ethnic groups from around the Nile River basin. They called them *Nilo-Hamitic.* Though both the terms Nilo-Hamitic and Hamitic are in use today to describe families of East African ethnic groups, they are, in fact, inaccurate and quite meaningless.

gated by wealth. In some sections of the city large mansions line broad suburban streets. They are enclosed by walls and protected by guards, called *askaris*, standing outside. These are the *mbwa kali*—"fierce dog"—areas. These neighborhoods were traditionally home to the European population, and remain so today, though some wealthy African Kenyans have moved in.

And there are neighborhoods of the poor, such as Mathare Valley.

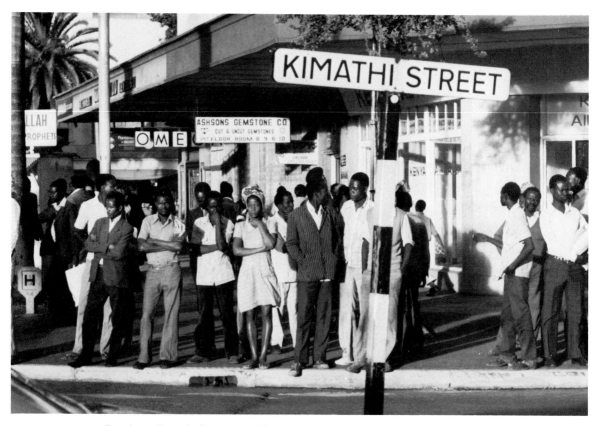

Crowds on Kimathi Street at midday. Shops in Nairobi's downtown are stocked with most modern consumer goods such as VCRs and microwave ovens, though few ordinary Kenyans can afford to buy what they see in shop windows.   Jason Lauré

Located on the outskirts of Nairobi, it is a shantytown where people have built homes out of cardboard and discarded bits of scrap. There is no running water, and open sewers line the dusty paths that serve as streets. There, all the inhabitants are Africans, of every ethnic group.

Religion is another division among Kenyans. Christians now account for 54 percent of the population and they are divided into Catholics, 16 percent, and Protestants, 38 percent. (The Protestant sects are also fragmented and competitive.) Moslems make up 6 percent of the population, and traditional religions, sometimes referred to as "animism" and based on belief in spirits and nature, account for about 40 percent.

The various traditional beliefs are different from area to area and sometimes from village to village. Oftentimes Kenyans combine traditional beliefs with Christian teachings, which results in the formation of Africanized Christian churches.

It is sometimes possible to tell where a person is from by the way he or she looks, speaks, or dresses. Many of the Masai, Turkana, or Somali dress in distinctive garb. But people from each of these groups might just as easily be found dressed in Western clothes and speaking English or Swahili. A man might wear a suit and tie while at his apartment in Nairobi, but choose traditional clothing while visiting in his home area.

Often, the division between ethnic groups is not clear. As people do

This mosque stands in the very center of Nairobi. Many members of Kenya's Asian community worship here. There are other mosques in Nairobi that serve Somalis, Arabs, and the rest of the Moslem community. Jason Lauré

in any country, Kenyans and Africans see themselves belonging to many groups. They identify with their family, their clan, their village, their town, their district, their religion, or their country, depending upon the circumstances.

Though it is not always apparent, a Kenyan's ethnic background still plays a very important role in his or her daily life. At times traditional ideas give way to modern concepts, and at other times the force of tradition dominates. But most often, tradition and change are merged into a culture that is both very modern and very African.

Couples in Nyayo stadium in Nairobi are married by Pope John Paul II during his visit in 1985. The Catholic faith is strong in Kenya and is also blended with traditional religions. Jason Lauré

Every Sunday in Kenya, Pentecostals can be seen running through the streets of many towns and cities in Kenya, banging drums and singing. This is one example of the merging of Christian and indigenous traditions. Jason Lauré

The Kikuyu

The Kikuyu are Kenya's largest ethnic group, numbering around 4.8 million people. Because they lived in Kenya's Central Province, around Nairobi and in the highlands, they had more contact with Europeans, missionaries, merchants, and colonial officials than any other group in Kenya. During colonial days it was the Kikuyu who lost the most land to British settlers, but it was also the Kikuyu who had some of the first and best opportunities to get British education, and to get involved in politics and commerce.

In general, they adapted most rapidly to European ways, religion, attitudes, and styles.

NOTE: The term *Kikuyu* is used here to describe the people as well as the language they speak and the land they inhabit. In many texts *Gikuyu* is used, and it is often considered to be more accurate. (The actual pronunciation is "Gekoyo.") *Kikuyu* is used in this text because it is more familiar to most Americans.

The Kikuyu are agriculturalists who live on small *shambas* located on the ridges and in the valleys around Mount Kenya. Since independence, many have acquired *shambas* on former colonial estates in the Rift Valley that have been divided among the landless. Many Kikuyu also grow cash crops: coffee in the highlands or pyrethrum, which is used as a natural insecticide, or sisal in lower-lying areas. Most own sheep, goats, and perhaps a few cattle if they can afford it.

Though the early Kikuyu left no written records, a rich body of myths and oral history was passed down through the ages.

In traditional Kikuyu belief, Mwenye-Nyaga was the creator of all things. Mwenye-Nyaga chose a man named Gikuyu to become father of the Kikuyu people. He brought Gikuyu to the snowy top of Kere-Nyaga, the Mountain of Light, and showed him the fertile land around the mountains, the streams, the valleys, the herds of animals. This land, Mwenye-Nyaga said, would be given to the Kikuyu people. Gikuyu was also given a wife named Mumbi, and they were told to go and populate the land that had been given to them.

Mumbi and Gikuyu had nine daughters, but no sons, so Gikuyu went to Mwenye-Nyaga for help and was told to make a sacrifice of a lamb. And when the sacrifice was completed, Gikuyu found nine husbands for

Kikuyu homes at the base of Mount Kenya. The round, mud-walled, thatched-roof design is traditional, but square-walled homes with corrugated iron roofs are becoming commonplace. N. Myers / Bruce Coleman Inc.

his daughters. They became the nine clans of the Kikuyu.

As the people spread, they began to divide into other groups. Some went to the north, and they became the Meru people; and others went to the south and were known as the Kamba. And others became the Embu.

Kikuyu legend also tells of their political history. According to legend, Gikuyu told the men who were to marry his daughters that he would grant them permission only if they would agree to accept a matriarchal system—that is, one dominated by women. They agreed. Each woman was permitted to have many husbands, a custom known as polyandry.

Soon, according to the story, the women became harsh rulers, forcing the men to work long hours and endure painful humiliation. The men revolted, overthrew the women, and established a patriarchal system. Polygyny—a system where one man can have many wives—replaced polyandry. And gradually a new government evolved that was ruled by a council of elders.

Kikuyu society was very individualistic. The Kikuyu were never one large, united group with a single leader. Rather, they lived in many smaller groups spread over a wide area. Though there were chiefs, they had little real authority. Decisions were made by councils of elders, who acted more as consultants than rulers. People were guided by their individual sense of responsibility to the group and to their own clan.

One of the most important studies on the Kikuyu people is the book *Facing Mount Kenya*, written by Jomo Kenyatta, who was later to become Kenya's first president, when he was a student in London. In that book, for the first time, an African described African customs and traditions from an African point of view. Where most Europeans regarded African traditions as barbaric, primitive, or quaint, Kenyatta's book treated them with respect and understanding.

A woman grinding grass to feed to her cattle in Meru district, Kenya. The cows were donated to a women's group by the U. S.-based African Development Foundation as part of a project to teach people to feed their cattle instead of letting them graze. Grazing cattle are responsible for much of the deforestation that has caused soil erosion in Kenya. By keeping the cattle penned up, farmers are also able to collect the manure for fuel and fertilizer. African Development Foundation

Other Bantu Groups

The term *Bantu* refers to a language grouping rather than to a cultural group. The language as well as the customs of the related Meru and Embu people are extremely close to the Kikuyu. While one travels through Kikuyuland, the language changes slowly until at one point it is called Kimeru, or Kiembu; but that line is not always clear, and Meru,

Embu, and Kikuyu people have little trouble understanding each other. The Meru now number more than a million by themselves and think of themselves as distinct from the Kikuyu.

The Kamba, who inhabit the drylands between Nairobi and the coast, are Kenya's fourth- or fifth-largest ethnic group, with over 2 million members. Their livelihood is diverse, now consisting of a mixture of farming and herding, though they were once known as hunters. And because of their proximity to the coast, they also became traders, forming a key link between their inland cousins and the coast. Other Bantu speakers include the Gusii in southwestern Kenya and the Luhya, who live north of the Lake Victoria region.

The Luhya are Kenya's second-largest ethnic group, with a population of over 3 million people. They, however, are more of a collection of related ethnic groups than a single, united group, which illustrates the difficulty in assigning ethnic labels to groups of people. The Maragoli people, for example, are considered to be Luhyas, though they themselves don't always agree, preferring to be considered a separate ethnic group. The Maragoli are the largest group under the Luhya umbrella. Other, smaller groups that are considered to be Luhya take advantage of the affiliation, which gives them influence and power as members of one of the largest ethnic groups in the country. The land the Luhya inhabit in western Kenya is some of the most densely populated in the world. Many Luhya, therefore, have found their way to Nairobi and other cities looking for work.

Luo

The Luo are the third-largest ethnic group in Kenya with just less than 3 million people. They live in the area around Lake Victoria and are known as fishermen, but that was not always the case. It is thought that the Luo migrated from Sudan in the 1400s, and were herders. They drove out the agricultural Bantu speakers from around the lake area and settled in. But over the centuries they have mixed with the Luhya, Gusii, and other Bantu agriculturists around the lake area, and many have become farmers, growing staple crops and sugarcane in the lowlands around the lake.

Their language, Jaluo, is similar to the languages found in the Nile Valley in Sudan and has nothing in common with the Bantu languages with which they are surrounded.

Before Kenya became an independent nation, they had very little to do with any of the groups on the eastern side of the Rift Valley, but independence found them thrust into a union with the powerful Kikuyu, and rivalries have developed for power and influence in independent Kenya.

Pastoralists: The Masai, Somali, and Others

The figure of the Masai warrior, tall and lean, face painted with red ocher, standing on a hilltop clutching a spear, is part of the image that many people have of Africa, even though the Masai are actually very few in number.

The Masai are pastoral people who live much as they always have in the open plains of East Africa on both sides of the Kenya-Tanzania border. The life of the traditional Masai very much revolves around their cattle. Cattle are the only real wealth they recognize, and they move to wherever conditions are best for their herds. In a country where people are hungry for land, the Masai have no desire to own any.

The Masai live in settlements called *bomas*, circles of huts made from

Young Masai morani *(warriors) performing a traditional dance. Their hair and faces are* *stained red with ochre, and complex patterns are drawn with white on their legs. The* moranis' *traditional seven years of survival training in the wilderness is now discouraged* *by the government, which prefers to see the young men in school.*   Jason Lauré

twigs and surrounded by barricades that hold their cattle in. Their traditional food is a mixture of milk and blood. The blood is drained from the necks of their cows and mixed with milk in a hollow gourd. The Masai very rarely slaughter their animals.

Traditionally, when a young man reaches the age of about fifteen, he is circumcised and becomes a *moran* or warrior. With their skin dyed red and their intricately braided hair also colored red with ocher, the groups of young *morani* are a magnificent spectacle. The *morani* then go off together and learn survival techniques. Some still take the traditional test of manhood by hunting lions armed with only a spear.

Masai herders on the move with their cattle. The Masai prefer to keep their wealth on the hoof. They rarely eat their cattle and migrate to meet the needs of their herds. United Nations / IDA / Pickerelle

More than most groups, the Masai resisted adapting Western ways, but the pressure of modernization in Kenya is forcing them to adapt. The *morani* once received their education by going into the bush for seven years; the government has now banned that practice and requires them to attend conventional schools. It is now illegal to hunt lions, and young *morani* may be as interested in getting jobs somewhere as the last generation was about caring for the herds. No longer can they trade cattle for everything they need. Kenya runs on cash, and the Masai need to make money.

Though many Masai still live a pastoral life in Kenya and Tanzania, they are trading on their reputations as fierce fighters by finding jobs as *askaris* (security guards) in Nairobi. Others perform traditional dances for tourists or make money by charging tourists for photographs.

Pressure on the Masai to change their ways also comes from farmers who are expanding their land under cultivation. Today many young Masai attend school, and intermarriage is increasing. But Masai tradition is strong, and even with integration into Kenyan society it is likely that the unique Masai identity will remain.

Other pastoral groups find themselves in similar situations. The Samburu are a branch of the Masai and live in the area north of Mount Kenya. The Rendille, Gabbra, and Boran are also nomadic groups who have slowly moved into Kenya from Ethiopia over the years. Many of these people are Moslem and have close relations with the Somali. These groups, living in Kenya's arid northern districts, also raise cattle but put a much higher value on camels.

Of all Kenya's ethnic groups the Somalis probably think of themselves as being the least Kenyan. One reason for that is the existence of the country of Somalia, the only country in Africa that is made up of a single ethnic group. For many years Somalia and the Somalis of Kenya's Northeastern Province had the dream of uniting that province with the Somali nation. A small guerrilla war erupted in the province during the 1960s, and Kenya held on to the territory. Since then, many Somalis have complained of poor treatment from the police and other authorities in Kenya. But that too may change. Now the head of Kenya's military is of Somali origin.

The Turkana people live along the western shore of Lake Turkana, inhabiting some of the most inhospitable land on earth. It is hot, often reaching 130 degrees, and there is little shade. The ground is dry and rocky, and water is scarce. The Turkana have become used to the famines that periodically descend on the land, wiping out herds and people.

An El Molo sharpens his spear. The El Molo are fishermen who live around Lake Turkana. Today less than 200 El Molo remain, as they marry into, and are absorbed by, the Turkana and Samburu people who also live near the lake.   The Hutchison Library

Like other pastoralists, they consider their cattle to be their wealth, and they take pride in their ability as warriors. In much of northern Kenya, for centuries, the different ethnic groups raided each other, stealing cattle and fending off reprisals. During colonial days the British succeeded somewhat in putting a stop to the raids, but it was later discovered that the constant mixing of cattle kept the herds healthy by diversifying the gene pool.

The Kalenjin

The Kalenjin are a large language group of more than 2 million people, made up of smaller distinct groups inhabiting the western Rift Valley. Kenya's president, Daniel arap Moi, belongs to the Tugen, a subgroup of the Kalenjin. The Kalenjin are thought to be related to the Masai, and some of the subgroups such as the Nandi and Kipsigis share many customs with the Masai.

The Nandi are perhaps the best known because of their fierce resistance to British colonialism. They strongly resisted attempts by the British to put the railroad line through their territory and had no fears about engaging the better-equipped British forces in battle. They also raided the Masai, stealing their cattle. The British mounted massive raids against the Nandi, killing thousands of young warriors and eventually pushing them into a reserve and taking their land for white settlers.

Forging a Common Heritage

Simple divisions between ethnic groups are also becoming obscured as

A Kipsigis girl, from western Kenya. The Kipsigis are grouped under the Kalenjin ethnic group. This type of traditional dress is becoming increasingly rare. AP / Wide World Photos

Age Groups

Traditional life among many of Kenya's ethnic groups was based on a progression through a series of age groups. An age grouping might include all the boys, or girls, born during a period of three or four years. The members of the group would together pass through initiation rites and together attain the status of adulthood. The age group replaced the calendar or solar year as a determinant of a person's age, and defined a person's behavior and role in the society. It was the glue that held the society together.

Nearly all of the tradition and ritual associated with the age groups was challenged by the European missionaries who came to Kenya.

BIRTH: The birth of a child was observed very closely by the midwives to be sure that everything was proper and that the spirits of the ancestors were not offended. A healthy birth was a cause for celebration. The birth of a girl meant wealth for the family because someday she would bring a bride price from her husband's family. If the baby was a boy, the mother would scream five times and the father, who was waiting in the fields, would cut five stalks of sugarcane. The boy child carried in him the spirit of the ancestors, creating an important link to the past.

The mother would carry the placenta to the family's field and bury it to assure that the land would be fertile. A sheep was killed, a feast held, and great quantities of alcohol consumed, with plenty poured on the ground for the spirits. The father would also be honored in the celebration, because the birth would promote him to a higher grade of elderhood.

In Kenya, as in much of Africa, the practice of infanticide was common. Twins were often left to die, as were, in some areas, children who were born feet first. Such births were regarded as bad omens. These practices, anthropologists now understand, also helped to contain population growth.

The killing of children was one of the first customs the missionaries successfully battled against.

CIRCUMCISION: With the exception of the Luo and a few smaller groups, all of Kenya's ethnic groups practiced both male and female circumcision. It was the first step into adulthood for both boys and girls. It came as they began to be sexually active, at about fifteen years of age. For girls it meant that they were women, and could marry and bear children. For the boys it meant that they had become warriors.

The rituals, carried out separately for boys and girls, were done with only cold water as an anesthetic, but the initiated were expected to show no sign of fear or pain. Dancing and feasting followed the ceremony.

The missionaries found the battle against circumcision more difficult than that against the birth rites. Their objection was mostly to female circumcision, which was a much more radical and dangerous operation than its male counterpart. It was not uncommon for young girls to bleed to death or die from infection after the operation.

As for male circumcision, the missionaries objected to the

dancing as much as to the operation. A compromise was reached, and the missionaries themselves circumcised some of the boys in mission hospitals. Today in Kenya males from many of the ethnic groups in more developed areas have the operation performed in the hospital under anesthetic and in sanitary conditions, though in outlying areas the traditional practices are still intact.

Female circumcision is less common today, but still widely practiced, and women's groups in Kenya have been working to stamp out the practice.

MARRIAGE: Many Kenyans still exchange a bride price as a symbol of the joining of two families. In rural areas that might consist of cattle and sheep, but in modern Kenya some fathers accept cash and checks for an agreed-upon amount. For many Kenyans today Christian weddings in churches have become the norm, but non-Christians from many ethnic groups still carry out traditional ceremonies of various types.

Polygyny still persists in Kenya, though it is less common than it was a generation ago. A man would traditionally marry as many wives as he could afford, and set each one up in a separate hut in his compound. The taking of additional wives meant higher status

conflicts arise between traditional cultural values and the fast-changing world of modern Kenya. Intermarriage among ethnic groups has created a generation of Kenyans of mixed ethnic heritage. And, slowly, many people are beginning to think of themselves as Kenyans.

But ethnicity remains an important element in modern Kenya and continues to play a large role politically and economically within the

for the man, and the first wife in the family enjoyed special status, if not always the most attention from the husband.

Christians were opposed to polygyny and tried to eliminate the custom, with only some success.

THE ELDERS: A final blow against the age-group system was the replacement of the traditional authority of the elders with the authority of the government. In many areas the role of the elders has been almost eliminated.

The abolition of important social practices has weakened the bonds between members of clans, age groups, and ethnic groups. As in the United States, where people decry the "decline of traditional family values," many Kenyans believe that they have lost something valuable, that youngsters no longer respect authority, and that their traditional societies are in decline.

But the changes have not been entirely negative. Women have benefited from the decline in female circumcision, all babies are cared for, and Kenya's central government has been able to help people in ways that would have been beyond the grasp of previous societies. And though many of the traditions themselves are dying out and evolving, new customs arise based on the old values.

country. Though Kenya's ethnic diversity can be a strength, resulting in a multifaceted national culture, these divisions have also created serious problems.

Kenya is very much a collection of individual groups and not quite the unified nation that was once envisioned. The problems associated with ethnic rivalries are called tribalism, and as a force it is as destruc-

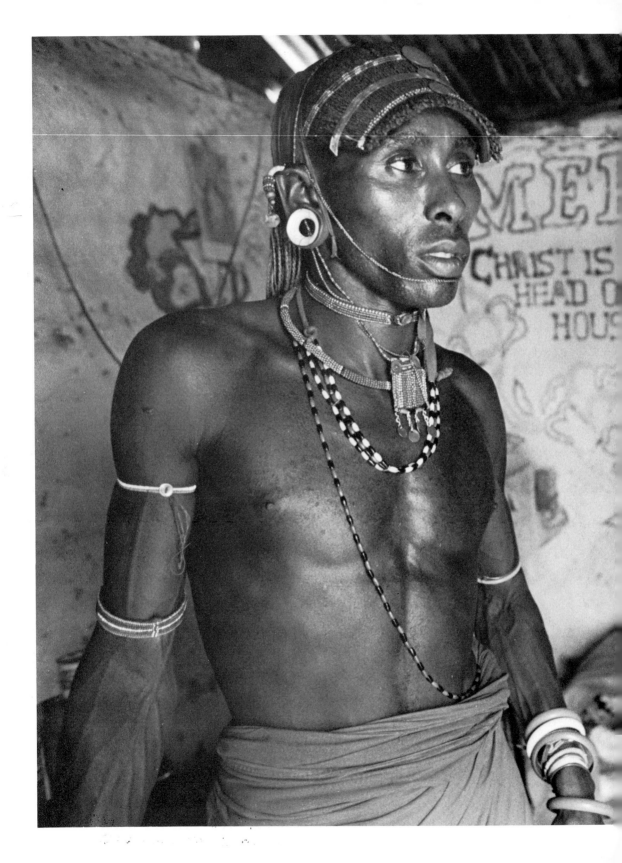

(Above) Three Samburu women walking home from church, wearing their Sunday best.
Amy Zuckerman

(Pages 54–55) This Samburu moran, *who spends most of his time in the wilderness, is visiting the home of a Christian relative in the town of Loiyangalini. Though families are often divided by lifestyle and the degree to which they accept Western traditions, the bond of family remains strong, and relatives from the bush are almost always welcomed by those who live in the town.* Amy Zuckerman

tive as the racism that exists in other countries today. Though Kenya's
rulers speak often of "stamping out tribalism" in order to weave these
diverse cultures into a single national entity, some politicians have
taken advantage of ethnic rivalries for their own political and financial
gain. Indeed, it is the politicians and leaders, not the people themselves,
whose actions usually result in tension among Kenya's ethnic groups.

Ethnic groups have also taken on new roles in modern Kenya, where ethnic identity can reflect regional economic interests as well. As in the United States, where different regional and ethnic interest groups compete for resources, Kenya's ethnic groups vie for resources such as roads, funds for education, and investment to provide jobs in their region. The representatives from each region who go to the National Assembly in Nairobi naturally put the interests of their constituents first.

It is only now that the first generation born in independent Kenya is reaching adulthood and coming into positions of prominence. The challenge for the young will be to mold themselves into one nation that will benefit from the multiplicity of proud traditions.

Early History

Imagine going into a history class and learning only about British history or Chinese history, about the kings and queens and emperors of distant and unfamiliar lands. Imagine that history textbooks talked only about foreign countries and never mentioned George Washington, Thomas Jefferson, or Abraham Lincoln.

This is the experience that Africa had for many years. The Europeans who ruled Africa denied that African history ever existed, and taught the students as if history began in Africa when the Europeans arrived only a few years before. In West Africa students in the French colonies were even taught that they were French.

In reality, Africa's history is as rich and complex as our own. It includes a succession of empires and heroes, times of war and times of peace and achievement. But since most of African history has been passed down in an oral tradition, much has been lost over the course of the centuries.

Much of what we know comes from legends, mixtures of fact and myth that, while holding much truth, leave large areas of doubt. There are ruins and evidence of great cities and civilizations: Axum, Great Zimbabwe and Meroe in East Africa, and Sohghai and Timbuktu in West Africa. But for now they leave more questions than answers.

Today there is increased interest in Africa's past. Historians and anthropologists are now helping to unearth bits and pieces of buried centuries. Western scholars, whose predecessors once attempted to deny that Africa had a history, are now contributing to this search. And as more African students complete university educations, they are beginning to delve into their own pasts to contribute to this growing body of knowledge.

Africa contains a wealth of untapped information, and as the pieces slowly come together a fascinating picture is beginning to emerge. And an important chapter is being added to the history of the world.

Prehistory

Charles Darwin was the first to surmise that modern humans originated in East Africa. Darwin's notions were at first laughed at when he published his *On the Origin of Species* in 1859, but one hundred years later the anthropologist Mary Leakey, working in Olduvai Gorge in northern Tanzania with her husband, Louis, unearthed some of the earliest hominid fossils ever found. (Hominids are human ancestors who walked erect.) The Leakeys called the discovery Zinjanthropus, or "man of Zinj," the name for the ancient East African coast.

The Leakeys later discovered *Homo habilis*, a contemporary of Zinjanthropus who was more advanced and used tools. Traces of *Homo habilis* are evident throughout the Rift Valley, including the area around Lake Turkana in Kenya, where their son Richard Leakey has done most of his work.

Then in 1974 Donald C. Johanson found what is to date the oldest hominid fossil known. The 3.5-million-year-old woman was found in Ethiopia, and he called her Lucy.

Though there is still much debate among scientists on the exact course of human evolution and on which of the ancient discoveries is the most direct human ancestor, it is widely acknowledged that East Africa is indeed the birthplace of the human race, the true Garden of Eden.

Today, many of the fossils the Leakeys uncovered can be seen at the National Museum in Nairobi.

Early humans roamed the open grasslands of East Africa, which today appear probably much as they did then. Looking across Kenya's open plains today, it is easy to imagine the first humans there, hunting, gathering, learning to use fire. These early people eventually learned how to domesticate animals and became pastoralists. It was then that they began to wander with herds in search of food for the cattle and spread themselves across the continent of Africa.

Kingdoms and Conflicts

Early African history is a swirl of human migrations. Pastoralists were constantly on the move, pushing hunter-gatherers off pastureland. Some of the pastoralists learned to cultivate and began settling in the Nile Valley. There, great civilizations such as Egypt, the Nubian kingdoms, and Kush sprang up. The center of Kushite civilization was at Meroe, where the Kushites developed their own script and built temples and palaces.

Around 1500 B.C., in Ethiopia, the city of Axum was in full flower. It was from there that some people believe the Queen of Sheba came before going to King Solomon's Jerusalem.

Farther south, in what is now Kenya, there may have been some contact with these cultures, but the extent of their interactions is not yet known. The inland areas there were probably sparsely populated by a few groups of hunter-gatherers. The first Bantu speakers who migrated to East Africa from central Africa probably originated somewhere in the area of modern Cameroon. They arrived about A.D. 500. From the north, the Galla, Gabbra, Somali, and others filtered into the area. While some of the Bantu speakers populated areas closer to the coast, the Kikuyu moved into the ridges around Mount Kenya, pushing out groups of Pygmies and the Wandorobo people who had lived there for centuries.

Around A.D. 1400 the Luo people came from southern Sudan looking for land and settled in Uganda and around Lake Nyanza (later to be called Lake Victoria) in Kenya.

While those who settled the more fertile highlands eventually gave up their pastoral life for agriculture, other groups living in the plains remained essentially pastoralists. By about A.D. 1500 the current population groups in Kenya were largely in place.

Trading relationships developed inland between the agricultural and pastoral people. Though the Kikuyu and other Bantu fought with the Masai, raiding each other to steal cattle and women, they also cooperated, trading goods and animals. Intermarriage was also common, and agreements were sealed with exchanges of women and cattle.

The Kamba people, who settled closer to the coast, became important traders and served as a link between the coastal and trading city-states there and the rest of the inland population. Goods from Arabia and the Far East often made their way inland, while ivory, rhinoceros horn, slaves, and other goods were sent to the coast from inland areas.

The Coast

The coastal areas were the site of a great mixing of populations: Arabs from the Arabian peninsula, Asians from the Indian subcontinent, and Africans from the north and from inland. The Swahili language evolved there from a mixture of Bantu grammar with many Arabic words. It was originally written in an Arabic script, and from those writings we get a clearer picture of coastal history.

A rich and vibrant Swahili trading culture evolved that was distinct from both its African and Arab origins. It expressed itself in unique architecture, cuisine, and customs, much of which remain intact today.

The coast's history is the story of competition and trade. Omani Arabs piloted small sailing ships called dhows along the East African coast, trading goods from one town to another, collecting gold from Zimbabwe, cloves and spices from Zanzibar, and bringing them to the Arabian peninsula. Then they would return with goods from as far away as China.

The trading towns became small city-states; Lamu, Gedi, Malindi, Mombasa, Kilwa, and Zanzibar (the last two are now part of Tanzania) were among the best known.

Each of these was controlled by Arab sultans from Oman, and each had its own army. For centuries, dating back perhaps as far as 2,000 years, these city-states cooperated or competed in trade and wealth. Power changed hands in cycles, and small empires rose and fell.

But these cycles came to an end in A.D. 1489, when a new power came onto the scene. That was the year in which Vasco da Gama and three Portuguese galleons rounded the Cape of Good Hope and arrived in eastern Africa.

Though da Gama sailed onward, the Portuguese returned seven years later with a fleet of warships. They attacked and plundered the island of Kilwa, then a major cultural and trading center on the East African coast, and demanded tribute from the sultans. Some of the weaker city-states joined in cooperation with the Portuguese while others resisted. The Portuguese established their headquarters on the island of Mombasa, where, in 1593, they built Fort Jesus, which still stands today.

After eighty years of battles the entire coast of East Africa from Lamu to Mozambique was under Portuguese control. Portuguese rule lasted about 200 years, ending in 1698, when Fort Jesus fell to the armies of the imam of Oman, sent from his capital in Muscat.

But the conflict over the lucrative trade routes continued, and there was no peace in the region. In 1746 the Omani settlers in the East African cities declared independence from the rulers in Muscat, and for almost 100 years the city-states of the East African coast, except for Zanzibar, remained independent from Muscat. But in 1837 the imam of Muscat reclaimed the East African states and moved his headquarters to Zanzibar, from where he ruled the East African coast as the Sultan of Zanzibar.

The power of the Arab sultans was to be short-lived, however. By the early 1800s Britain, now the world's premier trading nation, had its sights fixed on East Africa. The British military and British traders had become involved in the affairs of the competing sultanates, and were sought as allies in the constantly shifting military alliances.

And, also in the early 1800s, traders from a new nation, the United States of America, began sailing the East African coast. The Americans, in an attempt to break British monopolies on the coffee and tea trades, sailed directly to the Arabian peninsula. On their way home they stopped along the East African coast and traded nails, muskets, cotton, and wire for ivory, skins, and gum.

The Slave Trade

Though ivory, spices, and rhinoceros horn were important commodities for the early East African traders, slaves were the most sought after. The slave trade carried out by Europeans and Americans in western Africa and by Arabs in both eastern and western Africa is one of the great tragedies of human history and was a destructive and horrible force in Africa.

The Arab traders brought the slaves from central Africa to Zanzibar, where they were sold and sent on to Persia, Arabia, India, and possibly even China. At the height of the East African slave trade, 25,000 slaves per year were sold in Zanzibar's market. A few of them were sold to Europeans and ended up in the Americas. The Arab traders worked the coast and by the 1860s had moved inland in search of slaves, usually assisted by Africans, penetrating as far as southern Zaire. The Arab influence is still felt in southern Zaire, where the Swahili language is common today.

Many of the slaves taken in East Africa were not exported. They remained in the coastal towns, adopted the Islamic religion, and eventually became integrated into society there.

The Africans did not simply submit to the slavers without a fight. Though the Arabs were armed with modern and well-trained armies, several African leaders put up long and noble resistance. Among them the name of Manwa Sera stands out. For five years Manwa Sera battled the slavers, defeating the armies that they sent from Zanzibar. In 1865 he was finally captured and beheaded by the Arabs. After his death, other African leaders arose to battle the slavers.

It is the British, however, who must be given credit for ending the slave trade in Africa. By 1807 the British had abolished slavery in England and were determined to put an end to it around the world. Under pressure from Britain, the slave trade came to an end in East

Swahili, Kiswahili, Kitchen Swahili

Kiswahili is the term that one would use for the Swahili language if one were speaking Swahili. All languages belong to a class of nouns that begin with the prefix *ki-* and form the plural with the prefix *vi-*. English is therefore *Kiingereza*, and French is *Kifaransa*. To a speaker of Swahili the languages of other ethnic groups are *Kimeru*, *Kiembu*, *Kikamba*, and so forth.

Words referring to a person begin with *m* and form the plural with the prefix *wa*. Therefore a Kamba person in Swahili is a *Mkamba* and the group he belongs to is the *Wakamba*. Citizens are *wananchi* (*nchi* means country). A white person is referred to (sometimes derisively) as a *mzungu* and as a group are *wazungu*. There are many additional noun classes.

Perfect grammatical Swahili is generally what is spoken on Zanzibar and on the coast. Spoken in this fashion it is a poetic, alliterated language where adjectives and other modifiers take in the same prefix as the subject noun. Therefore, "The large book is on the table" is:

> *Kitabu   kikubwa   kiko   mesani*
> (book)   (large)   (it is) (on the table)

The plural would read:

> *Vitabu   vikubwa   viko   mesani*

(The word *mesa* is from the Portuguese.)

Many Kenyans who do not speak Swahili as a first language, however, are content just to communicate, and grammar is forgotten. Swahili words are mixed with the vernacular grammatical structures and, though the resultant sentences get the message across, many native Swahili speakers find it difficult to listen to.

One reason for this difference between the two types of Swahili is that Swahili is an easy language to learn and an extremely difficult language to master. The basic grammar contains rules that are rarely broken, and most people quickly learn a few phrases. More complicated structures quickly become confusing.

During colonial times the white settlers learned a few basic phrases and didn't bother really learning the language. They developed what is called kitchen Swahili, an abridged version of the language consisting of two-word commands that they would bark at their servants: sweep floor, wash clothes, come here, cook dinner, and the like.

The settlers took a kind of arrogant pride in speaking ungrammatically and mispronouncing words to make them easier on the British tongue. The most blatant mispronunciation of all is the name of the country. Many settlers called it Keen-ya, when it is in fact pronounced Ken-ya.

The irony behind kitchen Swahili is that most of the servants spoke English much better than the settlers spoke Swahili. The language was used as a way of keeping people in their place.

Africa by late in the nineteenth century.

Missionaries and Explorers

It was Christian missionaries who first began pressuring the British government to do something about slavery. Though the Portuguese had brought Catholicism to the East African coast, they had less interest in gaining converts than in controlling commerce. But the second wave of Europeans to arrive set out to convert Africans to Christianity while seeking a permanent presence in the region. They were Protestant missionaries from Scotland and Germany.

The first mission in East Africa began in 1846 under the supervision of Johann Ludwig Krapf and Johann Rebmann, Swiss German Protestants. Another missionary who was finding his way through Africa at that time was perhaps the most famous of them all, Dr. David Livingstone, the Scottish missionary and explorer.

Livingstone's aim was to bring commerce and trade to Africa. "Christianity and commerce" was his credo.

The missionaries were not very successful at turning the Moslem Swahili people into Christians, so they moved inland, where they enjoyed more success with non-Moslem Africans. Krapf, as was previously mentioned, was the first European to get as far inland as Mount Kenya, and he sent news of it back to Europe. With each successive foray to the interior, Europeans grew more curious, more interested in what riches the continent might hold.

As the missionaries moved into the interior, they began to enlist the help of European powers for protection and backing. Justifying their

Primary students in western Kenya learn to speak Swahili. For many Kenyans, Swahili is a foreign language. It is hoped that early schooling in Swahili will help young students to develop a sense of national unity. Yann Gamblin / UNICEF

NINETEENTH-CENTURY
COASTAL SETTLEMENTS
AND TRADE ROUTES

ARABIA

Muscat

Aden

Arabian
Sea

Surat
Bombay

Goa

INDIA

AFRICA

PRESENT-DAY
KENYA

Mogadishu
Brava

Malindi
Mombasa
Kilwa

SEYCHELLES
LAMU
ZANZIBAR

Mozambique
Quelimane
Sofala

Maputo

MADAGASCAR

MAURITIUS

BOURBON

Cape
Town

Indian Ocean

trips to the interior by saying that they had a duty to save souls, the missionaries opened the door to the eventual dominance of European political power in Africa.

At the same time, European scientific interest in Africa was increasing. The pressing question was the location of the source of the Nile, a subject of much interest and discussion since the time of the early Greeks.

Early explorers returned with theories, but no proof. A more organized effort to reach the headwaters of the Nile began in 1788, when the British African Association was formed.

In the mid-1800s explorers such as Sir Richard Burton and John Speke brought back tales of an inland ocean, the vast Lake Nyanza, later dubbed Lake Victoria by Speke, and of the Buganda kingdom, located in what is now Uganda, and of lands with untold riches.

When Speke saw the vast lake on August 3, 1858, he wrote, "I no longer felt any doubt that the lake at my feet gave birth to that interesting river, the source of which has been the subject of so much speculation, and the object of so many explorers."

Speke had no proof of his claim, and he was ridiculed by many of his colleagues. He died shortly thereafter, when the validity of his findings was still in doubt. It wasn't until 1875 that an adventurer and journalist from the *New York Herald*, Henry Morton Stanley, proved that Nyanza-Victoria was indeed the source of the mighty Nile.

None of the best-known explorers—Livingstone, Stanley, Burton, or Speke—actually traveled through what is today Kenya. Based as they were in Zanzibar, the most direct route for them to follow to the lakes was through what is now Tanzania. Nonetheless, their role in Kenya's history is as important as Christopher Columbus's in U.S. history, even though he never set foot on the American mainland.

Once the question of the Nile was settled, the Europeans embarked upon the task of finding the shortest route to its source. That route, they determined, would be from Mombasa and pass through the land of the Masai, whose reputation for fierceness was unsurpassed in Africa at that time. Most explorers chose to avoid them.

In 1882, the British Geological Society sent Joseph Thomson to test the hypothesis. Thomson, a Scottish naturalist and self-described wanderer, set out from Mombasa in 1883, trekking 3,000 miles in 14 months through Masailand, Kikuyuland, and Luoland to the shores of Lake Victoria and then back to Mombasa again. He came closer than any European had at that point to the peaks of Mount Kenya, and charted parts of the Rift Valley.

Thomson found the Masai to be relatively friendly, and his problems in passing Masailand had more to do with the fear the Masai generated among the members of his expedition than anything they did. In his frequent encounters with Masai *morani*, Thomson relied on his wit and sense of humor to make friends.

Though less well known than his predecessors, Thomson's importance as an explorer in Africa is unsurpassed. It was his efforts, more than anyone else's, that opened Kenya to the world.

The Scramble for Africa

The British appetite for exploration had been whetted by the early discoveries, but political developments taking place in Europe in the late nineteenth century would begin to make Africa increasingly important and launch what came to be called the scramble for Africa.

It was an age of imperialism, when governments worked to insure that they had trade advantages. European industries were in constant search of cheaper raw materials in order to gain a competitive edge, and they began looking to Africa and Asia for tea, sugarcane, coffee, and cotton, none of which grew in Europe.

With the opening of the Suez Canal in 1869, East Africa was no longer a distant outpost. It was on a major shipping route between Britain and its prized possession, India. At the same time rivalries between European powers for trade and influence were at a peak. France was claiming large tracts of territory in western Africa, and Germany had claimed land south of Kenya, in what is now Tanzania. The scramble was on as European powers moved to gobble up as much of the continent as they could lay claim to.

The Europeans' "ownership" of most of the African continent was formalized in 1884 at the Berlin Conference, where rules of exploitation were agreed upon, and where it was decided that European powers would work together to end the slave trade. But most important, it imposed upon the continent artificial borders, borders based on European interests and agreements rather than African realities.

Borders sliced ethnic groups in half and lumped into one administrative area diverse people who had little in common except that they were now ruled by the same power. Africa had been redefined in European terms.

The governments of these countries encouraged citizens to colonize as a method of holding down the lands in question. In 1895 the British established the East African Protectorate, which included present-day Kenya, Uganda, part of southern Somalia, and the island of Zanzibar.

Settlement

Britain's main interest in the region was Uganda. Uganda was lush, fertile, beautiful; and the Buganda Kingdom was one of the wealthiest in Africa. But Britain's interest in Uganda was also strategic, for there was the source of the Nile. The British had the idea that the country that controlled the source of the Nile would be able to control Egypt and the Sudan. Though British power was in place in Egypt at the time, they wanted to control Uganda to prevent a hostile power from blocking the flow of the Nile. England depended on Egypt for raw cotton for its textile trade, and the cotton depended on the Nile overflowing its banks at regular intervals and irrigating the land.

Though it is unlikely that anyone could have dammed the Nile in the 1800s, the British went on to consolidate their control of Uganda by building a railway from Mombasa to Kampala.

But building a railway in East Africa was not like building one in Europe. The engineers had little knowledge of what lay along the 675 miles between Mombasa and Lake Victoria. The explorers who had sought the source of the Nile had taken the shortest route and, therefore, most of Kenya was still a mystery to the Europeans even at the end of the nineteenth century. The railroad builders would have to learn about the geology and geography as they went along. The railroad was soon to change Kenya's history.

The building of the railroad got underway in 1896. Back in England it was being called "the lunatic line" and criticized as a waste of money. There was a problem getting workers. Africans from the coast refused to work, out of fear of the Masai, whose territory much of the rail line would cross. Wild animals and malaria also threatened. So in order to do the work, the British imported 32,000 workers from India—many of whom would later stay to become traders and merchants in the interior.

Three hundred miles from Mombasa was a place called Ngongo Bargas, a plain where Masai and Kikuyu met to trade. Caravans between Mombasa and Uganda rested there after either climbing out of the Rift Valley or preparing to descend into it. It was there that the railway depot that was to become the city of Nairobi was established.

As the railroad crept along, it brought with it settlers from England who began to claim land and begin farming.

In general, the Kikuyu, the Masai, and the British settlers got on very well, largely due to the influence of two chiefs: Chief Lenana, a Masai, and Chief Waiyaki of the Kikuyu.

There is some history of African resistance to the colonization, but

This advertisement from the 1920s reflects the attitude that Kenya was white man's country. Many Europeans regarded the Kenya colony as a playground for their amusement. Michael Maren

· 75 ·

The arrival of the railroad in Port Florence, as Kisumu was called by the British in 1900, was a triumph. The city was named after Florence Preston, wife of one of the railroad engineers. With her husband, she made the entire trip from Mombasa to Lake Victoria and drove in the final key of the railroad. By 1902, however, the port had reverted to its traditional name of Kisumu.   East African Railways & Harbours

the British were quick to respond with force of arms. In one particularly violent incident a British commander named Francis Hall moved north into what is called Muranga district with an army of Swahili soldiers from the coast and raided villages and butchered inhabitants in order to "pacify" the Kikuyu in that area. Farther inland the rail workers again ran into resistance from the Nandi people. But the British were determined to build an African empire, and they pushed onward.

In 1900 there were only 480 Europeans in Kenya. The Kikuyu didn't see them as a threat and didn't worry much when the whites started doing a little farming. But within fifteen years their number had grown to over 5,000, including 3,000 settlers who took large estates for themselves. The land-hungry Kikuyu began to realize that these strange white people meant to stay on their land.

This is how a young Kikuyu boy first heard of the arrival of the Europeans and the world beyond the forests:

On coming back from the coast the Kikuyu brought exciting news about what they had seen there. They talked about the big water, like a vast treeless plain, that stretched as far as the eye could see and beyond that. And how they had seen large animals that spat fire and smoke come floating on the endless water, and ghastly pale people coming out of these animals' stomachs. Their dress and behaviour was different from that of the Arabs, and they seemed to keep to themselves. The stories of these marvels from the coast were told and retold, and everywhere the people heard them with gaping mouths and staring eyes.

Many years later, as President of Kenya, Jomo Kenyatta would recall these childhood memories.

In 1909, Theodore Roosevelt was among those to ride the rails from Mombasa to Nairobi.
East African Railways & Harbours

Colonialism and Independence

Jomo Kenyatta's life spanned the period from the earliest days of white settlement well into the second decade of Kenya's independence. During those years he went from being a poor herdboy to the venerable position of the grand old man of Africa. And in many ways his life closely parallels the history of modern Kenya.

Kenyatta was born Kamau wa Muigai (Kamau, son of Muigai) sometime in the late 1890s, in the area now called Kiambu, north of Nairobi. His parents were ordinary farmers, and he had a traditional Kikuyu childhood. He tended the family's sheep every day with the other boys and learned Kikuyu history and customs from his mother at night.

His father died soon after his younger brother Kongo was born, and in accordance with Kikuyu custom, his mother became the wife of his father's brother, Ngengi. They had a son who was said to have been born with the spirit of the dead man and was given his name, Muigai. Shortly thereafter his mother died, and the young Kenyatta, at the age of about ten, was on his own.

From his friends he heard tales about the strange happenings beyond the ridges of Kiambu. He heard about the pink men and the iron snake that curled around the hills. One day upon his return to the village from watching the sheep he saw an excited crowd gathered around one of the strangers in his village. The stranger said that he was God's messenger.

The boy watched in amazement as the man read from a book while an interpreter translated for the people. Kenyatta looked at the black squiggly marks on the page and wondered how it was that the paper could tell the man what to say.

Kenyatta learned that the white men lived at a place called Thogoto beyond the edge of the forest. And in April 1909 the young barefoot boy clad in a goatskin registered at the Thogoto mission school.

It was a brave act of rebellion for a young boy, and even more frightening for a girl, to attend a mission school in those days. Many of the students came in defiance of their families. And it was common for fathers to come to the school to drag their children away. The elders accused the missionaries of breaking up their clans.

But the young Kikuyus were not abandoning their traditions. Many of them also wanted to attend the important circumcision rituals when it was time for their age groups to pass into adulthood. The missionaries stood firmly against the circumcision ritual for boys and were even more militant in their opposition to the ritual for girls.

When it came time for their age groups to become circumcised, many chose to defy the missionaries. Kenyatta was circumcised along with others in his age group, but in a slightly modified ritual. The tradition was usually accompanied with dancing and drinking and other acts that the missionaries disapproved of, and the operation was performed with a crude blade, but Kenyatta and some of the boys at Thogoto were circumcised in a more quiet ritual with a surgical knife.

He then returned to the mission to complete his Bible studies. Eventually he was baptized and took a Christian name. He was then called Johnstone Kamau.

The Kenya Colony

While the young Kenyatta was at Thogoto, colonists and missionaries were penetrating into the heart of Kenya. The twenty short years between 1895 and 1915 saw the wide-open African wilderness transformed into a British colony and brought under the control of a colonial administration.

Asian traders were setting up *dukas* (small shops) in villages, and young boys and girls were beginning to attend mission schools, where they were taught to read the Bible, first in their native language and later in English.

For the Africans it was difficult to tell the difference between the colonial authorities and the missionaries. A mission would arrive in a village and the colonial administration would soon follow. And both the colonial government and the missionaries issued a seemingly endless stream of instructions about what the Africans could and could not do.

As more settlers arrived and built their dreams on Kenyan land, the Africans began to see their heritage slipping away. Masai rangeland and Kikuyu farmland were fenced off into large European farms. The colonial government, under pressure from the settlers, caved in to their desire for more land on more liberal terms. Leases on the farms, originally for 99 years, were increased to 999 years. And the British administration ruled that even if Africans were living on a piece of land, they did not actually own it—a distinction that was totally alien to the Africans.

The British also imposed a tax system. It was a classic case of taxation without representation. The Africans had no say in the government and no idea what the taxes were for. And the Africans had no money. Theirs had been a barter economy. People traded what they had for what they needed.

In order to earn the cash to meet what was called the hut tax, Africans were forced to get jobs, at menial wages, working on European plantations. Indeed, a main purpose for the tax was to force the Africans to supply the labor that the European farmers wanted.

Men were required to carry passes, stamped by their employers and annotated with an employer's comments. If an African misbehaved, a note on the pass from an employer could make it difficult for him to get a job again. Without a pass, an African's movement was restricted to reservations that had been set aside for the African population.

Many Africans built huts and became squatters on their employers' land. Squatting allowed them to at least live with their families, but the employers often took advantage of this by getting the entire family to work. The system closely resembled the *apartheid* that exists today in South Africa.

While most Africans were placed on crowded reserves, 16,700 square miles (27,800 square kilometers) of the most fertile areas were set aside for white farms and were made off limits to any Africans who could not show passes that proved they had employment there. These areas were called the White Highlands.

It was in the White Highlands that the settlers planted their tea and coffee, fenced off huge ranches, and built their estates. Though much of the land remained undeveloped, the settlers had convinced the colonial government to ban Africans from using the land. The whites hoped

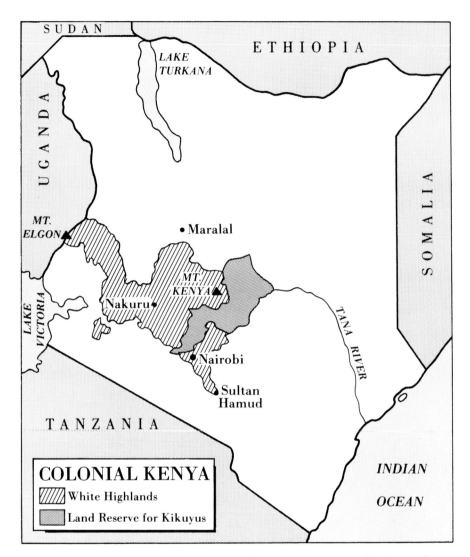

COLONIAL KENYA

///	White Highlands
▨	Land Reserve for Kikuyus

this would give them room to expand for generations. In those days, Kenya was called "White Man's Country."

The colonists who came to Kenya were mostly middle-class Britons looking for a new start in life, much like the pioneers who settled the

American west. Whereas in England they might have been middle-level clerks or civil servants, Kenya gave them the opportunity to be lords of their own land—but only at the expense of millions of Africans.

While Africans were confined to their reservations and being ministered to by white missionaries, the hypocrisy of the white man's world became apparent to them. Missionaries preached Christian morality and obedience to the Africans, but the settlers gained a reputation for engaging in drunken frolicking and sexual promiscuity. A white area on the edge of the Rift Valley was called Happy Valley by the settlers after the raucous activities that went on there.

Kenyatta would later observe that when the white man arrived in Kenya, he had only the Bible and the Kikuyu had the land. Then the white man taught the African how to close his eyes and pray, and when the African opened his eyes he had the Bible, but the white man had all the land.

World War I

With the Germans in control of German East Africa to the south, the beginning of World War I in Europe thrust Kenya into a colonial confrontation. Almost 250,000 Africans were pressed into service as members of the African Carrier Corps. Their job was to keep supplies moving through the hot lowlands of what was to become Tanganyika to the battlefront where the British and German colonists faced each other.

The British colonial force was formed of a ragtag bunch of settlers with hunting rifles and homemade uniforms. Asian troops were brought in from India to shore up the battle lines, but in the end it really wasn't much of a war. The two sides maneuvered and skirmished inside German East Africa while waiting for the real war to be settled in Europe.

In one telling incident the Germans mounted a raid to sabotage the rail line between Mombasa and Nairobi. Using highly inaccurate British maps, they became lost and never found the tracks. Finally the thirsty Germans surrendered, glad to finally get a drink of water and some rest.

Though the fighting was limited, the conditions for the African porters were horrible. The highland Kikuyu were not used to the tropical lowlands and came down with malaria, influenza, and other diseases from unsanitary conditions. In the end, perhaps as many as 50,000 Africans died for a cause that they really knew little about.

But Kenya's soldiers who returned had a new perspective on the world. They saw the folly of the European adventure in Africa and were less likely to be in awe of the white man. Many of the returning soldiers decided to start small businesses rather than return to the reservations, and these men formed the basis of a small middle class that would one day take an active role in the struggle for independence.

After the war, German East Africa, under its new name of Tanganyika, was ceded to Britain, along with parts of German colonies in West Africa. The British Empire seemed to be healthy and strong. More settlers arrived in Kenya, veterans from the war in Europe. More land was taken, now from the Nandi and other groups in western Kenya. And African agitation grew.

African Resistance

In 1920, in the district of Kiambu, a group of Kikuyu headmen came together for the first time to protest the taking of their land. Kiambu had become crowded with white farmers while the Kikuyu were being squeezed onto land that had been set aside for them. The British ignored their protests.

A year later an organization called the Young Kikuyu Association was formed. The head of the group was a man named Harry Thuku. Thuku, an employee of the colonial government, led protests over taxes and the pass system. And he traveled around Kenya trying to involve the Luo and others who had lost land.

The British reacted by jailing him. Africans took to the streets in protest outside the Nairobi police station. The police fired on the crowd, killing twenty-five Africans. Thuku was exiled to Somalia for a period of nine years.

But agitation for Africans' rights did not stop. In 1925 a group called the Kikuyu Central Association was formed. Three years later Johnstone Kenyatta became the head of the association. (He had taken the name Kenyatta after a Masai belt, a *kinyatta*, that he was fond of wearing when addressing rallies.) Once again the issue was land, and Kenyatta became the leading spokesman for the Africans' rights to their land.

In 1929 Kenyatta went to London to petition the British Parliament to allow Africans to be elected to the Kenya Legislative Council, which ruled the colony. His repeated requests were turned down, but he remained in Britain and Europe from 1931 through 1946 and worked for the rights of Africans in Kenya.

In Kenya numerous small organizations—many of them, such as the Taita Hills Association, dominated by a single ethnic group—had begun agitating for more rights. While their protests were centered on land, labor unions had also formed in the urban areas, voicing workers' demands for better wages and more opportunities for advancement.

Some of these groups were fired by a mixture of politics and religion, and they sprang from churches run by African pastors who preached a radical African brand of Christianity. The churches, once used by colonial powers to control the African population, now became the focus of dissent and rebellion. The African churches questioned traditional Christian teachings as well as the political authority of the British government and became a powerful force in organizing African political movements.

The Africans had taken the tools given to them by the Europeans and turned them into the instruments of their own liberation. The British had brought their education, religion, and ideas about democracy and freedom to Africa. The Africans had absorbed these gifts from Europe and integrated them with their own traditions. The word for freedom in Swahili is *uhuru*, and the idea of *uhuru* became the driving force in Kenya.

In 1940, as war once again had begun to engulf Europe, the British banned the Kikuyu Central Association, and its newspaper was shut down. Nonetheless, the African groups that were agitating for independence called a truce in their battle against Britain.

This time the enemy was the Italian armies to the north in Ethiopia and Somalia. As it turned out, the Italians never invaded Kenya, though the locals insist that they bombed the small town of Isiolo one night, thinking that it was Nairobi.

A crack African military unit called the King's East African Rifles was dispatched to guard the northern frontier. Other units of the East African Rifles were sent to fight the Japanese in the jungles of Asia, where they were given the most dangerous tasks and returned with numerous decorations.

Once again, returning soldiers proved to be a catalyst for independence agitation. The Africans reasoned that if they could fight and die for Britain, they deserved the right to vote and own land. By the time the war ended, Kenya was seething.

Leaflets like this one were dropped by the thousands into the forests where the Mau Mau were hiding. In English, Kikuyu, and Swahili, this leaflet promises fair treatment for any fighter who surrendered. Few if any of the Mau Mau took the government up on this.
AP / Wide World Photos

Ungikoruo wonia mundu o wothe wa Mbutu cia Ugitiri Bathi ino, niekumenya urenda kwineana na niegugutuga kuringana na kiiraniro giki kieru

MWIGITO WA KWIHONOKIA UKINEANA

THE BEARER OF THIS PASS WISHES TO SURRENDER. He is to be given fair treatment, food, and medical attention if required. He will be detained but he is **NOT** to be prosecuted for any offence connected with the Emergency which he may have committed prior to 18th January, 1955.

UYU UKUUITE "BATHI" ino arenda kwineana. Niatugwo wega, aheo irio na arigitwo angikoruo ni abatairio niguo. Ahingiruo na ndagacirithio ni undu wa uuru o wothe wa Mau Mau uria ekire mbere ya January 18, mwaka wa 1955.

ANAYEBEBA BARUA HII ANATAKA KUJITOLEA. Mpe msaada mwema, chakula, na atibiwe ikiwa anahitaji. Atafungiwa lakini hatashtakiwa kwa ajili ya uovu wo wote wa Mau Mau aliofanya mbele ya January 18, mwaka huu wa 1955.

GENERAL SIR GEORGE ERSKINE,
Commander-in-Chief.

SIR EVELYN BARING,
Governor.

Mau Mau

In 1946 Kenyatta, having abandoned the European name Johnstone and adopted the African-sounding Jomo, returned from England. In his absence a political party had been formed in Kenya—the Kenya Africa Union (KAU)—and in 1947 the leadership of KAU stepped aside so that Kenyatta could be elected president of the organization. In the same year India was granted its independence, and the idea of an independent Kenya seemed at last possible.

Kenyatta's followers at this time were mostly Kikuyu. But he began a crusade to link across the Kenya Colony. From the start there was suspicion. The Masai, Luo, and others saw him as a leader of the Kikuyu. And even some Kikuyu did not trust him. Many Kikuyu had done well under colonialism. This new elite supported the movements for more rights for Africans, as well as other changes that could help them in their businesses, but had no interest in pushing the British out. Younger Africans with less to lose, however, were becoming impatient, and the call arose for *uhuru sasa* ("freedom now").

Life had been growing steadily worse for the vast majority of Africans since the war. Unemployment was rising, and population pressure on the land was increasing—as were calls for self-government. White settlers continued to take over the Africans' land. It soon became apparent to many African leaders that the Europeans intended to stay in Kenya, that Africans might win a few rights by pressing for government reforms, but that Britain was not prepared to give up control of Kenya.

By 1951, African Kenyans had grown impatient. Protests began to get more violent. There were killings of cattle, and people refused to move from land as they were told. The British blamed the violence on a secret society that people had begun to refer to as Mau Mau. There are several theories about the origin of the term Mau Mau, but no one is sure which, if any, of them is correct. One view has it that the name was taken from the Mau plateau, where a group of Kikuyu farmers had resisted eviction by colonial authorities. Another possible explanation is that Mau was an anagram for the Kikuyu word for stop, and that people entering the guerrilla camps were told to Mau Mau, or stop!

Whatever the origin of its name, Mau Mau is best understood as the reaction of some Kenyans against the settlers' continued seizure of African lands. The Mau Mau fighters were a well-organized African guerrilla army. It was mostly a Kikuyu organization, though some Meru and Embu were recruited. Its targets were the European ruling elite and, more directly, the Kenyans who cooperated with the government.

The guerrilla army was united by a blood oath that all of them took. Among the Africans in Kenya an oath is not to be regarded lightly. The spilling of blood ties the oath taker to the land and to his ancestors. If a blood oath is taken, the oath taker will die before breaking it. To the Europeans this seemed like primitive magic, and they both condemned and feared it. Many Kikuyu and other Africans joined in the criticism of the oathing, fearing the fanaticism it might engender.

Rumor and fear spread about this secret society. The violence, which had begun slowly, escalated in 1952, when a chief who had been appointed by the colonial government was killed. Other attacks followed, and some white settlers were killed.

The government called a state of emergency and arrested Kenyatta for being a Mau Mau leader, even though he had publicly condemned the violence. He was to remain in prison for the next nine years. British troops were called in and more than 100,000 Africans were detained and thousands sent away from the cities.

But the Mau Mau warriors lived in the forests and swooped down at night. British propaganda tried to portray the Mau Mau fighters as a bunch of mad, half-naked savages terrorizing innocent victims. But if there was madness in the Mau Mau, there was also method. In one instance, with only five guns between them a group of Mau Mau fighters attacked the Naivasha police station and made off with truckloads of guns and ammunition. This was the work not of disorganized killers but of a well-trained army.

In reality it was the Mau Mau fighters who suffered the heaviest

A suspected Mau Mau is captured by the British police. The homemade gun the British officer holds is typical of the weapons that the Mau Mau fought with. The African soldiers, known as the Home Guard, did much of the fighting, and dying, for the British. AP / Wide World Photos

British paranoia and fear over the Mau Mau uprising led them to arrest thousands of Kikuyu at random in what was called "Operation Anvil." Here they sit at a concentration camp in Langata, outside Nairobi. AP / Wide World Photos

losses over the years of fighting, between 1952 and 1957. Only 32 Europeans were killed in the violence, along with 1,819 Africans who were considered to be loyal to the British. But more than 11,000 Mau Mau fighters died.

Kenyan politicians visiting Kenyatta at Lodwar in the spring of 1961. Despite the fact that his prison term had ended, he was being detained for "security reasons." Kenyatta is the bearded man with the cane in the center of the photo. Just to his right is Tom Mboya; and Daniel arap Moi, now Kenya's President, is the tall man second from left. On August 14, 1961, Kenyatta was finally freed and returned home to a hero's welcome.   Africa Report

The British had done everything in their power to focus attention away from the real causes of Mau Mau. But the continuing Mau Mau rebellion focused world attention on Kenya and brought home to the British what the rebellion was all about—the loss of African land.

In 1957 the British authorities began to give in to African demands. That year seven Africans were elected to the Legislative Council, and the next year seven more were added, making their numbers even with

Kenyatta is sworn in as the first Prime Minister of independent Kenya on December 12, 1963. His third wife, Mama Ngina, is on the left.   Kenya Information Services

the whites. In 1959, the laws that prevented Africans from living in the white highlands were repealed.

These concessions by Britain and the colonial government had been strongly opposed by the settler community. In 1949 the white legislature had published a document called *The Kenya Plan*, which stated that whites should be the dominant race in Kenya and sought to unite Kenya with the other white-ruled states in Africa: Rhodesia (which is now black-ruled Zimbabwe) and South Africa.

But by 1959 the tide had turned toward independence. The former colony called Gold Coast was now a country called Ghana, which had become independent in 1957; and British authorities were certain that Kenya would eventually follow. In October of 1959 a new Colonial Secretary, Iain Macleod, was appointed in London. Macleod was convinced that independence was at hand across all of Africa and that 60,000 whites in Kenya could not keep six million Africans from independence.

Not all of Kenya's settlers were completely opposed to granting rights to Africans. Most notable among them was Michael Blundell, a wealthy farmer and one-time cabinet minister who led a movement of liberal settlers and politicians called The New Kenya Group. The New Kenya Group advocated a multiracial government—but was not in favor of complete independence.

Blundell's group met with Macleod in London early in 1960 and, after long and difficult negotiations, came around to Macleod's point of view and agreed not to stand in the way of majority rule.

When Blundell returned to Nairobi, he was branded a traitor by other settlers and became the target of rotten eggs and tomatoes as well as threats.

Africans' demands for independence now became louder, and from across the country came the demand that Kenyatta be freed from prison. By April 1959 Kenyatta's sentence was completed, but the British authorities continued to hold him, moving him north to the remote district capital of Lodwar and later to Maralal. Finally, on August 14, 1961, Kenyatta was released. He returned a hero, now not only of the Kikuyu but of all the Africans in Kenya. By jailing him the British had inadvertently created Kenya's first nationalist leader. Two Luo leaders, Oginga Odinga and Tom Mboya, added their voices to the support for Kenyatta, and *uhuru* became inevitable.

By 1960 the Africans finally gained a majority of the seats in the legislature, and the colonial government announced that independence would arrive "soon." Two political parties were quickly formed, the Kenya African National Union, or KANU, and the Kenya African Democratic Union, or KADU. KANU was made up of Kikuyu and Luo, while KADU had the support of many of the smaller groups and the Kalenjin and Kamba. In February 1961 elections were held, and KANU won a majority of the seats in the legislature. Kenyatta, though still in prison at that time, was nominated for the presidency of KANU, and in October after his release he was elected KANU's president.

Tanganyika won its independence from Britain in 1961, and Uganda followed in 1962.

In Kenya the land question was still a block in the independence negotiations. The Africans wanted the settlers' land back; the British government agreed, but wanted to be fair to the European settlers who had invested time and money into building farms. It was finally agreed that the land would be purchased from the settlers by the new Kenyan government, and that the British government would lend it money to do so.

With that settlement came the announcement that Britain would finally be granting Kenya its independence. On December 12, 1963, the independent nation of Kenya was born.

The Fruits of Independence

Uhuru means freedom and independence. The very word was magic in Kenya. It lifted people's spirits and filled the new country with elation, confidence, and pride. Kenyatta was greeted with wild, ecstatic cheers wherever he went. He was the father of his country, like George Washington a living legend. They called him *Mzee* (pronounced m-zay), a Swahili term of respect meaning "the old man."

Kenya had reclaimed its birthright and taken back what rightfully belonged to it. Delamere Avenue, the main thoroughfare in Nairobi, named after one of Kenya's earliest white settlers, was changed to Kenyatta Avenue. The statue of Lord Delamere was torn from its pedestal, and a statue of Kenyatta was put up near the Parliament buildings. For the first time Africans could look and see a monument to one of their own. Kenyatta's picture replaced the queen's on Kenya's new currency, the Kenya shilling, and his portrait was hung in every shop and public place.

Other colonial names were also changed over the years. The town of Fort Hall, named after the notorious British commander who had butchered hundreds of Kikuyu at the end of the nineteenth century, was given the traditional name of the region, Muranga. The town of Thomson's Falls, named for the British naturalist and explorer who had "discovered" the area, reverted to the Kikuyu name of Nyahururu. Lake Rudolf, named for a Hungarian count by the explorer who had trekked there in 1888, became Lake Turkana, after the people who were living there. And today in Nairobi tourists and British Kenyans sit and sip tea at the Thorn Tree café on a street named after Dedan Kimathi, a Mau Mau leader who was hanged as a terrorist by the colonial authorities.

The promise of *uhuru* was that wealth like that of Britain would soon belong to the new nation of Kenya. The Africans saw that the British had become rich exporting Kenya's coffee and tea, and now it was their turn. People were eagerly awaiting the *matunda ya uhuru*, the fruits of independence.

But it wasn't to be that simple. When the independence celebrations died down, the new government of Kenya came face to face with serious problems. The wealth that had been distributed among the few thousand colonists in Kenya was not nearly sufficient for the millions of hungry Africans. The *matunda ya uhuru* that were available were very few, and competition arose over who would get the first taste.

Nationalism Versus Tribalism

Within the borders of the newly formed country were people who had never before considered themselves to be part of the same unit. Some,

A statue of Kenyatta is unveiled outside of the Parliament buildings, replacing the one of Lord Delamere. It was the first time that Africans were able to see a monument to one of their own. Kenya Information Services

like the Kamba and the Nandi, had never really had much to do with each other, while others, like the Kikuyu and the Masai, had been traditional rivals. At the time of independence it was clear that the Kikuyu were in the best position to lead the country and benefit from independence. In general they were the best educated, and their proximity to Nairobi put them in the best position to get government jobs.

Many of the smaller ethnic groups in the country feared domination by the Kikuyu and Luo, who had formed KANU, Kenya's ruling party. Some even felt that they would be treated more fairly under British rule than under independence. The smaller groups had formed another political party before independence—KADU, the Kenyan African Democratic Union—and among their leaders was a former schoolteacher named Daniel arap Moi.

The basic disagreement between KANU and KADU was similar to the one that existed between the large and small states in the early days of American independence. The larger ethnic groups, like the larger states, favored a stronger centralized government, while the smaller ones, fearing domination, wanted more regional autonomy.

Soon after independence, however, in the interests of national unity, and under some pressure, KADU was dissolved and the different groups decided to work out their differences within KANU.

Other disputes persisted. Ethnic Somalis living in Northeastern Province had requested that their area in Kenya become a part of Somalia. Somali leaders refused to vote in the 1963 elections, and armed groups, backed by the government of Somalia, attacked police stations and military outposts in a three-year guerrilla war.

Kenyatta preached against the evils of tribalism. "We are all Kenyans," he would say, and the people would cheer. But beneath the surface there was a growing mistrust, suspicion that some groups were favored over others. In addition, it was impossible to expect that hundreds of years of ethnic division would vanish overnight, that cultural differences would instantly no longer matter. The fact was that Kenyans still considered themselves to be Kikuyu, Luo, Kamba, or Nandi before they were Kenyans. Politicians seeking bases of support played upon the ethnic differences to create loyal followings for themselves, and ethnic tensions in Kenya were bound to become more intense before they relaxed.

Suffering Without Bitterness

Kenyatta spent the early months of independence assuring the former colonists that they were welcome to stay and work in Kenya so long as they became Kenyan citizens. Though many left, others decided to put their faith in Kenyatta, the man they once had accused of being a terrorist; the man they had expected to lead them "unto darkness and death."

Building the confidence of white settlers and the peaceful transfer of power was certainly one of Kenyatta's greatest achievements. The new Kenyan government bought 2,750 white farms for a total of $28 million in those early years. Most of those farms were distributed to the landless. Kenyatta also included former colonial officials in his first cabinet, and many colonial officials who had become citizens of the new state remained in their positions in the civil service, police, and armed forces.

Kenyatta's plan was to gradually "Africanize" as more Africans qualified to fill the positions. In contrast to other newly independent countries in Africa that dove blindly into self-government, Kenyatta planned to take things slowly.

He even showed forgiveness toward the colonial officials who had once locked him up, sometimes having tea with them and asking their advice on running the new nation. Kenyatta's pronouncements filled the

A tearful farewell. In 1967, Jomo Kenyatta declared that foreigners would need to have work permits for all jobs that Kenyans could do. Many Indians and Pakistanis employed in these jobs were forced to leave the country. Today in Kenya, many Asians still feel that their positions are precarious and that at any time they could be asked to leave.
AP / Wide World Photos

air: "Our aim is to bring all people of all races together." "There must be no revenge." "All of our citizens are equal under the law." These were the themes that were stressed again and again.

But Kenyans quickly became impatient. Kenyan troops in Nairobi complained about taking orders from the remaining white officers, and they became irritated with the slow pace of promotions for Kenyan soldiers. They mutinied, and British force had to be called in to quell the revolt.

Kenyatta's reliance on the former colonial master to secure his own power angered those who had fought the British for independence, and two distinct factions emerged in Kenya.

This photo of three boys in their school uniforms is meant to show the harmony that exists in Kenya. Asian, European, and African children do attend school together in Nairobi and Mombasa, but a great deal of segregation still exists outside the classroom. Rural schools are entirely African. Kenya Information Services

Mr. Double-O

Kenyatta's vice president was a Luo, Jaramogi Oginga Odinga—Jaramogi being a term of respect in the Jaluo language. Odinga had a large following among the Luo and Luhya people in Kenya, and he was the leading spokesman for those who felt that Kenya should pursue a socialist path. Kenyatta, who as a young man had spent time in Moscow, became increasingly anticommunist as time went on.

Odinga and the Luo felt that Kenyatta had given too much power to the Kikuyu, and in particular to Kikuyu from his own area in Kiambu. Odinga complained that land was not being distributed to the landless poor but accruing to the already landed rich among the Kikuyu.

Though Kenyatta and Odinga did not see eye to eye on these political matters, Kenyatta, for the sake of national unity, needed to keep a powerful Luo as his vice president.

Odinga was some twenty years younger than Kenyatta, and many assumed, and the Luo hoped, that he would one day succeed Kenyatta as president of Kenya.

Not all Luos were Odinga backers, however, and many Kikuyu supported his political positions, especially when he preached rapid Africanization and called for the casting out of colonial influences.

One of the most prominent Luos to support Kenyatta was Tom Mboya. A young man with ambitions of his own, Mboya was popular among all of Kenya's peoples. He was a labor union leader, a cabinet minister, and a good friend of the United States, where he often traveled and had many friends. He was also a rival of Odinga's for political influence among the Luo and one of the few non-Kikuyus to have Kenyatta's complete confidence.

Kenyatta had built a home on his ancestral homeland at Gatundu. There he held court with the Kikuyu "insiders," people from his own area who were his most trusted friends. Odinga and other Luos complained that the real government had been moved out of parliament to Gatundu, and that Kenya had not yet achieved real independence. In his book *Not Yet Uhuru*, Odinga complained that the colonial government was still intact, the only difference being that Kenyatta and his friends were now running it.

This concept is known as neocolonialism. Kenya, it was charged, was a neocolonial state because countries like Britain did not need to directly rule a country so long as that country continued to behave like a colony.

American and European business started moving into Kenya, and some Kenyans wondered if this could truly be independence if foreigners owned the country once again. They feared that the wealthy countries who had once taken Kenya by force could now just step in and buy the country.

Kenyatta and his followers believed that foreign investment would be necessary for Kenya to develop and that foreign business could provide jobs for Kenyans. Unlike some western and central African countries, which had exports of copper, gold, and other minerals to bring in money, Kenya relied on a few agricultural commodities such as coffee and tea. Kenya, they said, would need foreign investment if it wanted to industrialize.

Around Kenya today there are signs that Kenyatta got his way. Companies such as Hilton, Firestone, Union Carbide, and Del Monte were among the American companies to invest in Kenya.

But much of the money that foreigners brought into Kenya ended up in the pockets of Kenyatta's friends. Bribes were paid and shares of companies and directorships were given to the Kikuyu elite in order to insure the government's cooperation.

Odinga continued to speak out against this, while professing his preference for socialism over the capitalist path that Kenya was on.

The Kenyatta Conference Center, Nairobi. The designers of Nairobi's tallest building attempted to blend traditional African styles into the design for a modern skyscraper. Many international organizations use the center's facilities for meetings and special events.   Sue Pashko / Envision

In 1966 Kenyatta expelled Odinga and his allies from KANU, Kenya's only political party. Odinga resigned from the vice presidency and formed another political party, the Kenya's People's Union, or KPU. Twenty-nine members of KANU left to join Odinga.

For the next two years, Kenyatta and KANU tolerated the activities of the small opposition party, but in 1968 he cracked down. Odinga was arrested and charged with receiving funds from communist countries. Other KPU members were arrested or prevented from running for office, and Kenya became a one-party state in reality, though the consti-

One-Party States

Today in Africa one-party states dominate. Unlike the United States and other Western democracies, where two or more parties nominate candidates for positions, including president, one-party states allow tight control by a few party leaders. There are elections, but people vote from among the candidates approved by the single party. This allows a government like Kenyatta's to get rid of candidates even if they are popular, as was the case with Odinga.

African countries justify the one-party system by pointing out that political parties in Africa tend to split along ethnic, not ideological, lines—as indeed was the case in Kenya. They also claim that the democratic tradition is new in Africa, and that voters need guidance and protection from those who would use ethnic strife to further their personal political goals.

Critics claim that one-party states are not true democracies and that Africans are quite ready to make up their own minds about whom to vote for.

tution still said that opposition parties were permissible. It wasn't until 1982, when Odinga once again suggested that Kenya needed an opposition party, that Kenya's constitution was changed to make a second party illegal.

Once the antagonists were gone from government, Kenyatta embarked on a more explicitly procapitalist path, drawing power around him personally and ruling in the style of a traditional chief. *Mzee* seemed at times like a gentle grandfather but at other times like a ruthless dictator. Opposition and even criticism were not tolerated.

Outspoken Kenyans ended up in prison, and businesses and wealth became slowly concentrated in the hands of a growing, predominantly Kikuyu, middle class.

Government Structure

While the structures of Kenya's government were outwardly democratic, Kenyatta freely manipulated and circumvented the power of parliament whenever it suited him.

The Kenyan government was set up with a parliament made up of elected members from local districts, an independent judiciary, and an executive branch, but today the real ruling power is within the executive. Kenya's constitution was modeled after the U.S. constitution, with a system of checks and balances, but the government evolved during the first years to give more and more power to one man, the president.

The country is divided into seven provinces, each with a provincial commissioner who answers directly to the president. The provinces are divided into districts, then divisions, locations, and sublocations. This structure brings the president's control directly into the villages, where the heads of locations, now called chiefs, have taken over the roles of traditional chiefs. This system allows villagers to immediately address a chain of command that leads to the president's office, and it has made people loyal to the president.

The president is elected for a five-year term, and there is no limit to the number of terms he can serve. But since there is only one party and one nominee, there has never really been a presidential election in Kenya that was of any significance.

The president has the power to appoint his cabinet and his vice president as well as the civil service, the people who run the country on every level. As most of the people who are employed in Kenya are

Despite the existence of only one political party, Kenyans are enthusiastic about voting and turn out for boisterous rallies in support of their candidates. In this case the candidate is Phillip Leakey, brother of Richard Leakey and son of Louis and Mary. Phillip is the only European member of Kenya's parliament. Because many Kenyan voters cannot read, each candidate is identified by a symbol, here a key. At political rallies, supporters chant the name of the symbol as well as the candidate's name. The name and symbol appear side by side on the ballot. Jason Lauré

employed in government positions, this allows the chief executive a large amount of control and, therefore, the ability to keep people loyal to him.

The Kenyan parliament has become a forum for debate and a rubber stamp for whatever the president wants to do. Few members of parliament have the desire to contradict the president, and those who do have reasons to fear for their political futures.

Nevertheless, the system of government that Kenya has today allows the potential for much greater freedom, and many Kenyans prefer their system of government to the systems of their neighbors. Though Kenyatta curtailed the power of parliament, he often took his message directly to the people. One of the most effective ways he did that was through the *Harambee* movement.

Harambee

In Kenya, cries of "Harambee" (pronounced har-ahm-bay) can be heard wherever people are working. In the United States, if four or five people together want to raise a heavy object, they might together say, "One, two, three, lift!" In Kenya they would do the same thing by saying "HaaaraaaammBay!" lifting the object together on the last syllable of the word. *"Harambee"* became the national motto under Kenyatta, and symbolized the idea that people working together could help themselves and accomplish more than one person working alone. (*Harambee* is sometimes translated as "let's pull together.")

Kenyatta told the people that the government did not have the funds to build the schools, clinics, roads, and other things that the country needed. He encouraged people to raise the funds and donate the labor to do those things for themselves.

A *Harambee* fundraiser in a village or town is like a combination of a political rally and a county fair. The organizers of the events try to get as many of the most powerful politicians to attend as possible. The presence of the president or the vice president assures a big turnout and a lot of donations. If they are not available, however, a couple of well-known cabinet ministers will suffice. There is dancing and music, and lots of speechmaking.

A Harambee water project. These people have volunteered their time and money to bring water for drinking and irrigation to their village. Here they are laying the foundation for a water tank. The water will be piped into the tank from streams that run off Mount Kenya. African Development Foundation

As each politician finishes the speech, he or she will make a donation of his own money to the project that is being funded. The bigger the donation, the more popularity the politician will gain, and each tries to outdo the other to make the biggest contribution. The people in the village are also encouraged to follow the example of their leaders and give as much money as they can afford.

Over the years millions of shillings have been raised and thousands of projects completed. Unfortunately, many schools found themselves without teachers and hospitals without doctors, though the government has been trying hard to staff these local institutions by training Kenyans and by supplying volunteers, including members of the U.S. Peace Corps, from abroad until there are enough qualified Kenyans.

The *Harambee* program gave the people in Kenya the feeling that they were building a nation for themselves. It inspired nationalism and civic pride as well as, unfortunately, a degree of local corruption. Over the years many local leaders took advantage of the fund-raisers to enrich themselves, and cynics said that, in Kenya, self-help really meant "help yourself."

Still, the spirit of *Harambee* survived as a monument to the desire of Kenyans to build their communities and their nation.

More Problems

But the spirit of *Harambee* could not hide the deep wounds within the country. On July 5, 1969, Tom Mboya was assassinated in Nairobi. A Kikuyu was captured and hanged for the crime, but whether he did it, and who ordered the killing, remain a mystery. Many people have theorized that in 1969, as Kenyatta was becoming old and sick, some Kikuyu feared that Mboya would succeed him as president. If there was one thing that the forces around Kenyatta did not want, so this theory goes, it was a Luo president, so they had him killed.

Whatever the truth is, Mboya's death opened up ethnic wounds within the country. Kenyatta appealed for calm and for an end to tribalism, but his pleas were met with stones and shouts.

Kenyatta tried to appease the Luo by traveling to Kisumu for the opening of a hospital that had been built with Soviet donations. But supporters of the KPU shouted him down. Finally, a frustrated Kenyatta turned to Odinga, who was sitting on the rostrum, and said, "We are going to crush you into the floor."

As Kenyatta's motorcade drove off, youths began throwing stones, and the president's bodyguard opened fire. At least eleven people were killed that day, and some seventy-eight people were wounded. Kenyatta's guards went around and confiscated film from journalists and tried to erase the incident from Kenya's history.

But the Luo never forgot. And Kenyatta never returned to Kisumu again.

Another blot on Kenya's history was the murder of J. M. Kariuki. Kariuki was a flamboyant member of parliament who had once been detained under the state of emergency during the Mau Mau period. In the early 1970s he became the most outspoken critic of Kenyatta in parliament, and his popularity among students and the *wananchi*—the common people—was rising quickly. His criticism of the government for corruption and nepotism attracted crowds and cheers.

But in March 1975 he was abducted by police and murdered. Someone tried to burn his face off with acid, and his body was left for the hyenas. But the hyenas stayed away from the faceless corpse, and the body was discovered. The murder of Kariuki prompted others in the government to raise their voices, but one by one they were forced to resign their positions.

Kariuki's popularity underlined public dissatisfaction with Kenyatta's government and impatience with the corruption and the vast landholdings of Kenyatta's closest associates, known as "the family." Many government officials were spending more time making themselves rich than helping their own people.

But *Mzee* was still respected. It was still remembered that he was the one who had suffered for independence and brought *uhuru* to Kenya. As he grew older, Kenyans were prepared to wait for the next government to distribute some of the *matunda ya uhuru.*

The Death of Kenyatta

There were many positive aspects to Kenyatta's presidency. The stability and confidence that he engendered made Kenya one of the most economically successful countries in Africa—although little of that wealth was ever shared. And Kenyatta held together a union of peoples that many experts predicted would never last.

His final years were filled with the expectation of his death. Kenyatta sometimes seemed in perfect health and at other times appeared to be a sick old man. Those around him started to position themselves to succeed him in office.

Under the constitution, the next president would be the vice president, Daniel arap Moi. Moi was thought to be a weak character, appointed to the post of vice president as a compromise. He was not a Kikuyu, which the Luo would never have tolerated, and he was not a Luo, which the Kikuyu would have objected to.

In the late 1970s a movement called the "change the constitution movement" sprang up. It was made up of people from Kenyatta's inner circle who wanted to prevent Moi from becoming president. They probably would have succeeded had it not been for Attorney General Charles Njonjo, a close ally of both Kenyatta and Moi. Njonjo saw to it that a law was passed making it illegal to speculate about the president's death. The debate was ended, and the wait began.

News about Kenyatta's declining health was kept from the public. Right up until the end Kenya's two daily papers showed *Mzee* doing something nearly every day: greeting diplomats, opening new schools, attending celebrations of Kenya's holidays, and dancing with traditional dancers.

On August 23, 1978, the old man finally died in his sleep, and Moi assumed the presidency. What at first was reported to have been a

Traditions That Die Hard
in Modern Kenya

S. M. Otieno was a modern Kenyan in every way. He was a well-known criminal lawyer. He wore expensive three-piece suits, lived in a wealthy Nairobi suburb, and drove a Mercedes-Benz. Otieno was a Luo who had little use for the old customs and often renounced them as outdated relics of a time gone by. In 1963, the year of Kenya's independence, he married Virginia Wambui, a Kikuyu. Otieno thought of himself as a Kenyan first. He never even taught his children the Luo language.

In December of 1987 Otieno died of a heart attack brought on by stress. Immediately the Luo people said that they wanted to bury him in traditional Luo fashion back in Otieno's ancestral land in western Kenya. Otieno's widow fought back, saying that his family had no right to the body and that she wanted to bury him in their family plot in Nairobi.

The dispute was brought before a Nairobi court, and the case quickly captured Kenya's and the world's attention. Kenya's

smooth succession turned out in reality to have been a close call for the new president. A secretly trained force was sent out to kill Moi before he could reach the state house, but the plot failed. Those behind the plot gradually declared their loyalty to Moi.

Moi was officially elected president in October 1978, and he pledged to Kenya that he would follow in the footsteps of Kenyatta—*fuata nyayo* in Swahili. He also asked that Kenyans follow in his footsteps, and

newspapers ran daily transcripts of the hearing, and American and European papers also took interest in this case of modern versus traditional customs.

Kenya's legal system takes into account the individual laws of the country's ethnic groups. The courts have been instructed to be guided by these traditional laws.

Luo law says that the widow has no rights over the property of her husband. But for Otieno's clan there was much more at stake than property. They believe that unless a Luo man is properly buried, his spirit will haunt his relatives, causing auto accidents, bad dreams, and birth defects.

Otieno's widow and children said that to award the body to the clan would be giving in to tribalism. Wambui, who has worked for women's rights in Kenya, said that it was a battle over the right of a woman to her husband's property.

At the end of a five-month court battle the judge in the case sided with Otieno's clan, saying that he was required by law to respect the traditional laws of the people. And S. M. Otieno was laid to rest in western Kenya according to Luo law.

"*Nyayo*" (footsteps) became the new rallying cry, replacing "*Harambee.*"

Moi released political prisoners and promised a new era of freedom in Kenya. He cleaned up corruption and promised new land-distribution programs. He began to replace Kenyatta's loyalists with his own men. But charges of corruption were soon leveled against Moi, and Kenya's economy failed to improve. The numbers of landless people were still on the rise, and dissatisfaction began to spread.

On the morning of August 1, 1982, a group of air force personnel captured the radio station in Nairobi and two military bases. They announced that a coup had taken place. "The economy is in a shambles and the people cannot afford food, housing, or transport," they broadcast over the radio.

People in Nairobi took to the streets and looted Asian-owned shops. Their frustration was apparent. Troops loyal to the government eventually overcame the rebels, shot the looters, and quelled the revolt.

Though the coup attempt did not have wide popular support, it certainly exemplified the tensions in the country and the feelings of frustration of many Kenyans. The coup prompted President Moi to tighten his grip on Kenya's political structures. He clamped down on the country's independent judiciary by claiming for himself the right to fire any judge who disagreed with him. Church leaders opposed this attack on the legal system, and when some of them spoke out, Moi threatened to take away the people's right to freedom of religion.

Some twenty years after *uhuru*, poor Africans were still begging in the streets of Nairobi, watching rich Asians, Europeans, and a new class of rich Africans—called *wabenzi* in recognition of their favorite car, the Mercedes-Benz—dining at outdoor cafés and living the good life.

Kenya has made some strides in its quest for prosperity, but there is still a long way to go before the expectations that came with *uhuru* are reached. Today, a second generation, born in independent Kenya, awaits a taste of the *matunda ya uhuru*.

An Education

It is one week before the national school examinations in Kenya. For seventeen-year-old David Nkonge, the four-day-long test could determine the course of the rest of his life. He will be tested in math, geography, biology, physics, English language, Swahili, religion, and literature. He will be expected to know about the significance of the Tennessee Valley Authority, the Magna Carta, the Berlin Conference, and the Mau Mau rebellion. He will have to know sines and cosines, and be able to calculate the volume of a cylinder. He will be asked to interpret Portia's speeches from Shakespeare's *The Merchant of Venice*. He will be asked to draw a diagram of the circulatory system, calculate the specific gravity of several elements, and cite chapter and verse from the Bible.

Primary school children outside their school in western Kenya. Children still attend school barefoot in most rural villages. Kenya has increased dramatically the number of children able to attend primary school in recent years by paying for schools and teachers even in the most remote villages in the country. Marc Sommers

David's story is typical of thousands of young Kenyans today: He was born in a mud hut less than a hundred yards away from the spot where his school, the Ngeru Secondary School, now stands, and he still lives there with his parents, four brothers, and two sisters.

The village of Ngeru is located in Kenya's coffee country, high up on the fertile eastern slopes of Mount Kenya in Meru district. The regular rains and rich volcanic soil assure that food is plentiful and that people's basic needs are cared for. As a small child Nkonge worked on his father's coffee *shamba*, pulling weeds from around the coffee trees and helping with the harvest of the dark-red berries when they were ripe. With his brothers he helped his mother prepare the soil by hand and plant the maize and beans that make up the family's staple diet.

Every morning he and the older children would walk down a steep hill to a stream and return with buckets of water balanced on their heads. His mother would use the water to cook maize meal porridge, called *uji*, over an open fire in the family compound. She would also use it to make the morning tea. She would sprinkle some on the mud floors of the houses in the compound to keep the dust down, and some would be used for washing. It seemed to David that he was always walking up and down the hill, fetching water.

He would also tend to the goats and the one cow that his family owned. This was work reserved for young boys in the village. Every evening he would slide back the thin tree branches that penned in the cow, and he would untether the goats from the various places around the family compound where they were tied. And then, cracking a stick against the ground and shooshing air between his teeth, he would drive the animals to the stream below for water and to some open pastureland half a mile from his family compound.

Upon his return, his mother would dish out a thick, steaming, white maize meal cake called *ugali*, which she would cover with beef broth containing vegetables and, on special occasions, chunks of meat.

Schooling

There was a primary school in the village. It had been started by a local church and taken over by the Kenyan government at independence in 1963. Few of the parents in the village had ever attended school, and like Nkonge's parents, most could not read or write.

When Nkonge was six years old he became the first person in his family ever to attend school. After his morning chores he would walk barefoot down a path between the coffee trees with the other young children to attend classes in the mud buildings that served as the classrooms.

There, Nkonge was taught to write in his own Kimeru language. But he was also taught Kenya's two national languages: Swahili, which is spoken throughout the country, and English, which he would have to learn well if he wished to succeed.

Kenya's school system is modeled after the British system. The students attend seven years of primary school, standards 1 through 7, followed by four years of secondary school, forms 1 through 4. Once the students reach the first form, all their classes are taught in English. The exams they take after finishing the fourth form, the ones that David is now preparing for, are called the O (for Ordinary) levels. And the students who do well on those may gain admission to forms 5 and 6, which are about equivalent to the senior year of high school and first year of college in the United States.

After form 6, the students prepare for A-level (for Advanced-level) exams, which determine if they will gain acceptance at one of the technical colleges in Kenya or join the very best students at the University of Nairobi.

Until 1974 parents had to pay school fees for their children to attend primary school. The government simply did not have the funds to pay for books and teachers' salaries. Most Kenyan families did not have the money to pay the relatively high fees. Many students ended up attending school for a few years but had to stop if, for example, there were a drought and the family didn't earn enough money from the sale of their crops. Often families had only enough money to send one child to school, forcing them to make difficult choices.

In 1974, however, the government announced that it would pay for the first four years of primary school. National enrollment shot up from 1.8 million students to 2.7 million. In 1979 all fees for primary schools were abolished and enrollment climbed to 3.7 million. By 1980, around 95 percent of Kenya's children were attending primary school, among the highest percentage in all of Africa.

When David was in primary school there was no secondary school at Ngeru. At independence Kenya had only a few secondary schools, and many of them were considered to be as good as the best secondary schools in Europe. But for students in small villages like Ngeru there was only a slim chance that they could do well enough on the exams to qualify for the few places available in the schools. Most of those positions went to students from the cities and towns.

In cities such as Kisumu and Nairobi, or towns such as Meru and Nyeri, students live much as an American student might. They have television, libraries, and well-equipped primary schools with plenty of books and teachers. In addition, many of the students in the towns have parents who come from different ethnic groups with different languages. Their common language, therefore, is English or Swahili; and those are the languages the children speak, giving them a significant head start in school.

In contrast, the Ngeru parents, like the parents in many small villages, can speak only the local dialect and can provide very little assistance to their children.

Very few students from Ngeru ever reached the secondary school level. And across all of Kenya today, only 20 percent of students are able to attend secondary schools. But in many villages, such as Ngeru, that number is rising quickly.

The Ngeru Secondary School is what is called a *Harambee* school. In the middle of the 1970s the parents of the village of Ngeru came together and decided to build a secondary school so that their sons and daughters could continue with their education. The farmers in the village pooled their money and bought some land. They donated their money and labor and constructed the four classrooms that would contain forms 1 through 4. They also built two dormitories and a dining hall out of corrugated iron sheets.

They raised funds to buy books and hire a headmaster and some teachers. (And even after that contribution the parents are required to pay school fees for each of their children in attendance.) The total costs were enormous, and even more significant in light of the fact that students at the government schools could attend for free. But such was the commitment the parents of Ngeru—and parents in hundreds of other villages in Kenya—made to the education of their children.

For Nkonge the new school at Ngeru provided him with a second chance. Though he had tried hard in primary school, he did not do well on the exams. When he returned home after school, there were chores to be done. Sometimes in the evening, young David would have a little time to look at his schoolbooks by the flickering yellow light of a kerosene flame within the mud walls of the hut he shared with his family.

Even though Nkonge lived only a minute's walk from the new school, he moved into the boys' dormitory. The headmaster, Mr. Kangoori, said that he wanted the students to live at the school and not be distracted by the chores that would confront them at home. Also, keeping the students together on the school grounds would allow the teachers to enforce one strict rule at the school: The students must speak only English or Swahili. Anyone found speaking the local Kimeru language would be sent to fetch five buckets of water from the stream below.

The dormitories are not what an American might expect to find. There are two—one for boys, the other for girls—and each is one long room with a mud floor. Inside, two long rows of bunk beds are crowded against the walls. Meals are served in the dining hall, another long building with a mud floor, a few tables, and no chairs. For breakfast the students get *uji* every day.

After breakfast, the day begins with an assembly around the flagpole. The students, wearing their blue-and-gray school uniforms, stand with their classmates as the national anthem is sung and Kenya's flag is raised. This is followed by announcements and the assignment of daily chores. The students are expected to care for the school grounds, wash the floors of their classrooms, and fetch the water that the cooks use to prepare meals. Classes begin when the work is done.

Nkonge shares books and a desk with other students. But when he was in form 1, he even had to share a chair with another student. The school has no library and no science lab. There are about fifty to seventy-five students crowded into each class. And every year the form-1 classes are getting larger.

Some of the teachers at the school aren't much older than the students, and a few have gone only as far as to complete the exams for which the students are now preparing. But there is a shortage of teachers in Kenya, and many would prefer to teach in government schools. Recently the Kenyan government has agreed to pay the salaries of some of the teachers at the *Harambee* schools, which has saved the school some money and improved the quality of the education.

Kenya is also graduating about 7,000 teachers every year from schools such as the Kenya Science Teachers College and Kenyatta College, but they are having trouble keeping up with demand.

In contrast, some of the government schools are much closer to what might be found in developed countries. Some have broad lawns with stately buildings for classrooms and modern facilities. Some even have gymnasiums and stadiums.

Soon Nkonge will sit for the same exam that the students from the government schools are taking. He knows that his chances are slim, but like many students from the villages, he feels that it is worth the chance. In reality, only a few of his classmates will pass and go on. Of those who don't pass, a few fortunate ones will have enough land to raise their own families. The girls who don't pass will hope to get married to a man who has a job, or to one who has some land.

Dim Prospects

Many of the students who pass the exam, but who don't do well enough to gain acceptance to higher levels, will move on to the towns and cities looking for work. But there is not much work available in Kenya. Experts predict that by the year 2000 fully 40 percent of Kenya's work force will be unemployed. Those most affected will be people who, like Nkonge, come from small, crowded villages where there is little land available.

Graduation day at the University of Nairobi. Nearly 9,000 students are enrolled at the University of Nairobi and its affiliate campus, Kenyatta College. Graduations like this one have become rare, as student protests against government policies result in frequent closings of the schools. Jason Lauré

A popular novel, *Kill Me Quick* by Kenyan writer Meja Mwangi, tells the story of Meja and Maina, two young boys who finish school and go to Nairobi looking for work. As the book opens, Meja and Maina are searching through garbage bins for food.

"I came out here raw and proud the way you are," Maina said to Meja, scraping away the side of an orange. "I thought I would get a job and earn six–seven hundred shillings a month. Then I would get a house, a radio, good clothes and food. . . .

"Well I tried to get a job," he said and shrugged. " 'What qualifications?' they would ask me. 'Second Division School Cert . . .' I would start to say, but before I had finished the man behind the desk would roar, 'Get out, we have no jobs.' "

What Maina was trying to tell the man was that he had achieved a second division on his exams, meaning that he had passed with good grades, but not good enough to enter form 5.

The book follows the two boys through the streets of Nairobi as they beg for work and finally are forced to steal in order to survive. Sadly, it describes how both boys have left behind in their villages proud families who expected that they would succeed because of their education.

The students in Nkonge's class are reading *Kill Me Quick*. It will be one of the books that they will be tested on in their exams next week. But as they sit through review classes and study every night by the dull light of kerosene lanterns in their classroom, the message of the novel is something they need to know to answer questions on the literature exam, and not, they hope, a prediction of things to come.

Today Kenyans are looking at their education system and instituting some reforms. They have realized that the British system is not appropriate for a poor, developing country like Kenya. For if a student should return to the *shamba*, the education in Shakespeare, history, and alge-

Women's Work and Women's Rights

The women walked slowly but steadily, barefoot over the hot, rocky ground, talking quietly among themselves. They were not old, but their faces were worn and tired-looking. All of them were bent slightly forward, and into each of their foreheads was pressed a rough sisal rope. Each rope stretched back across a woman's shoulders and was tied to a ten-gallon can of water, which she balanced on her lower back.

A woman can easily stand up straight and carry a bucket of water on her head, but because it is four miles between the river and the village, these women carry as much as they can in one trip. In Kenya, carrying water is work for women and children.

Women also do most of the farming in Kenya. They plant and care for the maize and beans. If the family is fortunate enough to have coffee, they weed around the coffee trees. If the roof of the family's house needs to be rethatched, it is the woman who might walk fifteen miles with a hundred-pound bundle of straw tied to her back. In addition to this there is the cooking, the laundry, giving birth, caring for the children, and buying or selling food in the market.

It is the man, however, who controls all the money and handles selling the cash crops. And, most significantly, the man owns the land. In some cases a woman has no rights at all to the land, even if she has

bra will not be of much use. What is needed there perhaps is training in agricultural techniques, skills in carpentry or in managing livestock. Some of the students, whose parents have the money, will be able to go on to school to get these skills.

For the others, and for this entire generation of young Kenyans, there are many questions not yet answered. David Nkonge's children will

worked it for years. Her husband, if he so chooses, can divorce her and leave her with nothing.

Some studies have estimated that women do 80 percent of all the work in Africa but receive almost none of the money. While men are allowed to spend the family money on beer or on a new radio, women have very little control of where the money goes. Some experts in the field of development now think that this state of affairs has held back economic growth in many African countries.

Though Kenya's record on women's rights is not good, there are some signs that things are beginning to change. Girls in Kenya now have an equal opportunity to attend school. Parliament has debated the issue of women's right to own land, and there has been more sympathy for the women's cause. Several women have been elected to parliament, while a few have begun to succeed in business.

A strong organization, the National Council of Women of Kenya (NCWK) is helping to promote a network of women's groups across the country. The women's groups are teaching women skills such as reading, bookkeeping, health and nutrition, agriculture, and carpentry.

Because women own no land they have no collateral for getting loans from banks. Now some of the women's development groups have started giving small loans to help women start their own businesses and decrease their dependence on their husbands.

probably not know the same life that he has known on the *shamba*, in a peaceful little village. Whatever the results are on his exam, he will be moving on, to another school, to a job in a town or in Nairobi, or perhaps to no job at all and a life of troubles. But for now Nkonge is hoping, and studying hard for his exams.

Arts and Culture

Kenya's cultural heritage can be found in dances, songs, stories, and intricate and ornate body painting. These were once much more than crafts and entertainment. They were integral elements of the culture of each ethnic group, defining values and society and giving people a role in the universe. Passages such as births, circumcisions, or funerals occasioned grand celebrations and brought an ancient heritage to a new generation. But now, sadly, much of this has changed.

The Christian missionaries who came to Africa to convert and the colonial officers who came to control were horrified by the dancing and the rituals. The colonial government rewarded those who acted in a fashion that was more British than African. The missionaries preached a gospel that equated Christianity with Western values. So-called Christian names adopted at baptism were in reality only English names.

Circumcision rituals were ended. Dancing was stopped, and people covered themselves with trousers, shirts, dresses and other Western-style clothes.

Across all of Africa a process of Westernization took place that challenged many of Africa's traditions; replacing or blending them with foreign and strange notions that Africans could not completely accept. The result was a cultural confusion that has yet to be resolved. The influx of Western values can be viewed either as a tragic destruction of an old culture or the inevitable evolution that all societies experience. American traditions, for example, have altered dramatically from generation to generation. We do not celebrate Christmas and Thanksgiving exactly the way our grandparents did. Some might call this a loss, but culture cannot stand still in a changing world.

Those Kenyans who still cling to the customs of the past—some of the Masai, Samburu, Turkana and others—are relics of a time that in years is not so distant but seems far removed from modern Kenya. Kenya today is a country where Levi's, three-piece suits, fast cars, and expensive imported cigarettes are symbols of status.

Teenagers listen to Western music on portable tape players. In Nairobi, young Kenyans play video games in arcades and watch *Dallas* on television at night. People flock to theaters to see *Rocky IV*, *Star Wars*, or the latest James Bond film. Most American films reach the theaters here only three or four months after their release in the United States. The government sends trucks with electric generators and movie projectors to the villages. Kung-fu films are particularly popular in the rural areas. And when people speak of theater in Nairobi, they usually mean whatever plays have been recently imported from England.

To these "modern" Kenyans, the traditional Turkana or Samburu are sometimes regarded as an embarrassment, a reminder of a dim and "primitive" past.

The Europeans and Asians who live in Kenya have imported their own cultures and adapted them to the Kenyan environment. The Asians listen to their own music. Several movie theaters in Nairobi show only films from India. Asian restaurants are everywhere, serving up curries, *chapatis*, and other foods from the East. Many of these foods have become common in the Kenyan diet.

There are plenty of restaurants catering to Western tastes, including the Lord Delamere Room at the colonial Norfolk Hotel, a blatant reminder of Kenya's colonial past. Pizza parlors and Chinese, Japanese, and German restaurants are also found in Nairobi. Often the only Africans seen in these places are the waiters. The African sometimes seems out of place in his own country.

Today in Kenya traditional dances are performed for tourists at game lodges in the evenings, at events honoring Kenya's national holidays, or by schoolchildren to entertain visiting dignitaries. Carvings done by Kamba craftsmen and sold to the tourists are not of traditional design but are only an expedient way to earn cash. The Masai and others mass-produce spears, knives, and other implements they once took great care to make.

These dances and crafts, separated as they are from their original purpose, have traded away much of their traditional meaning and taken on a mostly commercial significance. But the performances also allow some Kenyans to preserve parts of their heritage in changing times.

Literature and the Oral Tradition

Kenyans have a great oral tradition. The storyteller was a respected

A mother in traditional dress and her more modern daughter in the tiny village of Lorugumu, in the Turkana district of northern Kenya. The influence of new ideas and fashions can be felt throughout Kenya, even in the smallest villages. Julia Ann Odom

person whose words could weave a binding spell while his stories transferred values and culture to a younger generation. In the oral society a person was respected for his wit and his ability to capture an audience for many hours at a time.

Many of the stories had animals as the main characters. Among the Kikuyu and other ethnic groups across Africa, the hero of many a story was the hare, the animal that would outwit the stronger and more ferocious hyenas and lions. Some of these stories from Africa reached the United States through the slaves and evolved into the popular Bre'r Rabbit stories.

Ngugi wa Thiong'o, Kenya's best-known writer, remembers the stories he heard as a boy, particularly the "suggestive, magical power" the language had. The tone of the words, the nuance, and the sounds were important parts of the art of storytelling. And none of that can be translated, for it was part of the Kikuyu language.

Ngugi recalled:

And then I went to school, a colonial school, and the harmony was broken. The language of my education was no longer the language of my culture. . . . English became the measure of intelligence and ability in the arts, the sciences and all the other branches of learning. English became the main determinant of a child's progress up the ladder of formal education.

Kenya today, like Kenya under colonial rule, puts little value on vernacular languages. To get ahead in modern Kenya a person must speak English. Kenya's writers write in English as a way to be understood across the country and across the world. Likewise, writers in the former French colonies of West Africa feel that they must write in the French language to have a wide audience. Many of Africa's writers and artists abandoned the cultures they came from. As a result the local languages have grown stagnant, and the people who speak only the local languages have been abandoned.

But that has started to change. In 1977, Ngugi wa Thiong'o, who had published many novels and plays in English, decided that he would write literature only in the Kikuyu and Swahili languages. The English language, he said, had colonized and taken over the minds of Africans as surely as the colonial forces had taken the land of Africa. He began to write and stage plays in the Kikuyu language. And that was when his troubles with Kenya's government began.

Ngugi wa Thiong'o

From the publication of his novel *Weep Not Child* in 1964 through his best-known work, *Petals of Blood*, published in 1977, and numerous plays and essays since then, Ngugi has written about social and political issues. His novels were the literature of protest and were part of an African tradition of using the power of words in poetry and song as a weapon against one's enemies. During the Mau Mau, for example, fighters composed poems and songs mocking their enemies, the church, and the chiefs who cooperated with the British.

Among Ngugi's plays was *The Trial of Dedan Kimathi*, which glorified the executed Mau Mau leader and exposed British hypocrisy during the trial that convicted him. But it didn't take Ngugi long to begin criticizing the new Kenyan government, which he perceived as being dominated by neocolonial interests. Over the years those criticisms became harsher and bolder.

So long as Ngugi wrote in English, the Kenyan government tolerated his criticisms. He was professor of literature at the University of Nairobi, and his novels were popular and widely available in Kenya's bookstores. His last novel in English, *Petals of Blood*, tells the story of poor villagers oppressed by a government that is under the influence of foreign corporations.

It was clear to all who read the novel that Ngugi was talking about Kenya under Kenyatta's government, but most Kenyans could not read the book.

But later in 1977 Ngugi staged his play *Ngaahika Ndeenda* ("I Will Marry When I Want") in his native Kikuyu tongue, for the first time reaching a much wider audience. The play was performed at the Kamiriithu Community Education and Cultural Centre, an experimental theater built by the local community to involve the audience in discussion of the cultural and political issues raised by the play. Ngugi was jailed.

In 1978, after Kenyatta's death, he was released as part of a general amnesty granted by the new government of President Moi, but he was not allowed to return to his post at the university. His prison diary, *Detained*, became a best-seller in the short-lived time of freedom during the early years of the Moi government.

But in 1982 the government once again began to crack down on dissent. After another of Ngugi's plays, *Mother Sing for Me*, was performed at Kamiriithu, the center was demolished by the Kenyan authorities, and Ngugi fled to Britain.

Even in exile Ngugi remains a focus of the government's anger. In 1987, as internal opposition to Moi's government was rising in Kenya, Ngugi was accused of being the leader of *Mwakenya*, an underground organization that was said to be trying to overthrow the Moi government. Most people found the charges ridiculous, but Ngugi has been told that he will be jailed if he ever returns to Kenya.

From London, Ngugi remains the voice of modern Kenyan literature. His efforts to use and expand African languages are the beginnings of a movement to redefine Kenya's cultural identity.

Music

The songs and poetry of protest have not become a part of Kenya's popular music, which usually deals with the less controversial subjects of love and romance. When musicians have a message, it is usually in praise of leaders, and because the government runs the only radio station in the country, that can be an effective way for a band to get music on the air. Some music has been used for social purposes, such as promoting the virtue of having small families.

Most modern Kenyan music is a combination of traditional rhythms and Western rock sounds played on electric guitars. (The Western music from which Kenyans borrow has its own roots in the African music brought to the Americas by slaves that later evolved into gospel, blues, jazz, and rock.) The vocals are based on the traditional mode of having a chorus of voices respond to a leading solo voice, the same "call and response" format as is now found in American gospel music. The lyrics are generally in Swahili, though sometimes English or local languages are used and are often mixed together in the same song.

Much of Kenya's traditional music is grouped under the name *ngoma*. *Ngoma* refers to a drum that was used among many of the Bantu-speaking peoples who used drums as the central instruments in their music. Each ethnic group had its own type of *ngoma* music and used its own language in the songs. This is the music that was used in rituals, and it is still possible to hear it in many parts of Kenya. In addition, some of this music in now available on records in Kenya.

Kenyan music is most often heard, and sometimes sounds best, crackling out of a small speaker in a shop or in the back of a *matatu*. Along River Road in Nairobi, where there are many African shops, the sounds of the music being broadcast by the Voice of Kenya fills the air from hundreds of small radios hanging on the street.

Nairobi is packed with clubs where the bands play and discos where people dance to Western music in rooms filled with pulsating lights. People dance and drink all night. Many of the clubs where the Kenyan bands are playing are packed almost exclusively with Africans. Others draw a mixed crowd. The most popular bands that play in these clubs are from Zaire and Tanzania.

While music from western and central Africa has reached the United States—King Sunny Ade, Fela, Franco, and Alpha Blondy, for example—Kenyan-style music has failed to catch on here.

Sport

Outside Kenya the country is perhaps best known for its great runners. Kenya's prowess in running came to the world's attention in 1968 at the Mexico City Olympics, when the small, newly independent African country competing in its first Olympic games took home three gold medals, four silvers, and two bronze.

Kipchoge (Kip) Keino won the gold in the 1,500-meter race, beating the American Jim Ryun. Naftali Temu and Amos Biwott took the gold in the 10,000-meter run and the 3,000-meter steeplechase, respectively.

Keino, a policeman, and Temu, an army private, both had little formal coaching and training. Unlike those in the more developed countries, especially those in the Soviet bloc, where young athletes are discovered and nurtured at an early age, few of Kenya's schools have athletic programs. Many young and gifted athletes never have the opportunity to develop their talents.

In more recent years many of Kenya's athletes who have succeeded on an international level have received coaching and education at universities in the United States. Ibrahim Hussein, who won the 1987 New York Marathon, attends the University of New Mexico.

In the 1988 Olympics, in Seoul, South Korea, Kenyan athletes once

Ibrahim Hussein crosses the finish line as the winner of the 1987 New York Marathon, while New York's Mayor Ed Koch holds the tape. Roderick Beebe

again put on a dazzling show on the track, sweeping most of the long-distance races. Runners Julius Kariuki (3,000 meter steeplechase), Paul Ereng (800 meters), Peter Rono (1,500 meters), and John Ngugi (5,000 meters), all trained at U.S. colleges, won gold medals. In all, Kenya took home nine medals, including two in boxing, an impressive display of athletic power from so small a country.

Football (soccer) is the most popular organized team sport in the country. It is played in newly built Nyayo Stadium in Nairobi and on rutted former maize fields in rural areas. Kenya's national team competes in the Pan-African Games and in World Cup competition, though teams from western and central Africa have tended to dominate international competition on the continent.

(Above) Football (soccer) is the most popular sport in Kenya. Teams are found in most schools and towns, and many companies and organizations sponsor teams. Kenya competes internationally with other African countries and in the Commonwealth Games, which bring together athletes from Britain's former colonies. Amy Zuckerman

(Right) Paul Ereng wins the 800-meter race in the NCAA championships for the University of Virginia in June, 1988. Later that year he went on to bring home a gold medal in the 800 for Kenya in the Olympics. R. M. Collins, III

For many in Kenya, sport still means the games of the British gentleman: horse racing, hunting, tennis, cricket, billiards, squash, and the like. The colonists built sports clubs in most small towns that allowed them these diversions. It is still possible to get up a game of squash in many Kenyan towns, but few Africans play. During colonial times the Africans were banned from these clubs, and today they serve as social clubs for the few remaining former colonists, the Asian busi-

Cheetah devouring the remains of an ostrich in Samburu National Park. Hunted for sport and their skins, the cheetah are joining the ranks of endangered species. Jason Lauré

Kenyan savanna stretching from horizon to horizon. The lines divide and then converge again, forming a never-ending procession as they walk, hop, and sometimes thunder across the Masai Mara Game Reserve toward the Serengeti Plain in Tanzania. They plunge into rivers and gallop over boulders on a frenzied, endless journey in search of pasture. The wildebeest are in a constant migration, following the rains, and when the massive herd passes through Masai Mara in August and September, those who are fortunate enough to view the spectacle gaze in wonder.

Sprinkled among the wildebeest are other members of the gazelle

ness community, foreign aid workers, and some wealthy Africans who enjoy the trappings of colonial power.

In Nairobi, horse racing still draws large crowds of Europeans—old men with handlebar mustaches, khaki shorts, and walking sticks—who can, for an afternoon, bask in the old colonial glory. Many of them still manage to live lives that have little relation to the problems and realities of modern Kenya—and sport plays a large role in this illusion.

One other sporting event, which has been controversial in Kenya, is the Safari Rally. This three-day automobile race was formerly called the East African Safari because the drivers raced through Kenya, Tanzania, and Uganda. When relations soured among the three neighbors, the route was confined to Kenya. Every year the rally draws large crowds along rural routes to watch the cars slog through the mud and negotiate the unpaved back roads of the countryside. Young children often stand on hillsides and entertain themselves by throwing rocks at the cars as they roar by.

Over the years several spectators have been killed when cars spun out of control, and this has led to calls to put an end to the rally. Most of the drivers are European, and the rally's opponents think that even one death is too high a price for Africans to pay for the Europeans' amusement.

But the race goes on, and the debate continues, as the race also earns substantial income for Kenya. Not even sport in Kenya is free of the remnants of colonial influence and the charged political controversies of the present.

Safari

A lone wildebeest stands on a hillside, munching grass and flicking at flies with his tail. This strange creature looks something like a cross between a bison and a cow. Its head seems too big for its body. Its unkempt, scraggly mane hangs across its neck and back like a tattered shawl. Its spine slopes downward toward spindly hind legs that are shorter than its forelegs.

The wildebeest lacks the sleek lines of the gazelle; the fleet, nimble grace of the impala; or the quiet sulking power of the Cape buffalo. Individually they are dowdy beasts, not the favorite subjects for tourists' photographs, except when they are being eaten by lions.

But when a migration begins, the wildebeest are a sight to behold. Hundreds of thousands of them form long lines that wind across the

Cheetah devouring the remains of an ostrich in Samburu National Park. Hunted for sport and their skins, the cheetah are joining the ranks of endangered species. Jason Lauré

Kenyan savanna stretching from horizon to horizon. The lines divide and then converge again, forming a never-ending procession as they walk, hop, and sometimes thunder across the Masai Mara Game Reserve toward the Serengeti Plain in Tanzania. They plunge into rivers and gallop over boulders on a frenzied, endless journey in search of pasture. The wildebeest are in a constant migration, following the rains, and when the massive herd passes through Masai Mara in August and September, those who are fortunate enough to view the spectacle gaze in wonder.

Sprinkled among the wildebeest are other members of the gazelle

Giraffe Manor, in the town of Karen, near Nairobi. This private home, owned by a British Kenyan resident, has attracted many tourists to pet and feed the domesticated and rare Rothschild giraffes.   Jason Lauré

family—impala, Thomson's gazelles (called "tommies"), eland, and topi—in a marvelous procession of creation.

At a watering hole within hearing distance of the hoofbeats, zebra, elephants, and buffalo stand side by side. Small white birds, egrets, stand on the backs of the buffalo picking insects from their hides. The buffalo, squinting and oblivious, just wade in the mud. In a nearby stream a hippopotamus raises a massive head from the water and snorts. Crocodiles sunning on the banks glance in her direction.

A giraffe stands by an acacia tree delicately picking slim leaves from between sharp thorns. A family of elephants lumbers into a wood, where an old bull stops to rub his back against a tree trunk, in Amboseli park. Across the border the snowy dome of Kilimanjaro (it is redundant to say Mount Kilimanjaro—Kilima means "mountain" in Swahili) looms above, and it appears close enough to reach out and touch.

A bush pig, its tail sticking straight into the air, scoots through the tall grass. A leopard drags a small gazelle up to a perch in a tree. A lioness stretches out on a warm rock and watches her cubs as they frolic in the grass below.

This was big-game country, where Ernest Hemingway and, before him, Teddy Roosevelt went on hunting safaris. Each of them set out on foot from Nairobi with lines of African porters to carry their supplies and their guns. Today hunting has been banned and people arrive in cars and buses, but the land is the same and the wildlife that so enthralled the earliest visitors continues to amaze visitors.

In the evening the lions (*simba* in Swahili) grow hungry. The single wildebeest standing away from the herd continues to nibble at the grass. Three lionesses fan out across the base of the hill, while a fourth makes a wide loop and emerges from behind the startled wildebeest. The wildebeest turns and gallops down the hill right to the spot where a second lioness is waiting. She rises on her hind legs and with a clean swat of one big paw brings the wildebeest to the ground. The others arrive quickly, followed by the cubs, and all join in the feast. A thick-maned male who has been watching the action from the side now moves in and pushes some of the cubs aside. Overhead, vultures coast across the evening sky, riding warm columns of air and only occasionally pumping their massive wings.

Lions seem to pay no attention to tourists and photographers who come very close to them in cars. They do pay considerable attention, however, to people who get out *of cars.*
Steven Greenfield

European tourists visiting the Lake Turkana region photographing Samburu morani. *The Samburu and others who wear traditional dress pose for pictures and usually charge tourists for photographing them.* Amy Zuckerman

As the lions eat hungrily, a convoy of yellow buses circles the kill. The tops open and tourists poke their heads and cameras out and begin clicking away. The lions don't even look up. Then, as quickly as they have arrived, the yellow buses speed off in a cloud of dust, looking for a rhino or a leopard or some more elephants before it gets too dark.

Tourism

The jumbo jets landing at Jomo Kenyatta Airport come from London, Frankfurt, Zurich, Athens, Paris, and Rome, bringing tourists on safari to Kenya. They come to visit Kenya's game parks—Amboseli, Tsavo, Masai Mara, Meru, Samburu, Marsabit, and others. Each of the parks contains several hotels, tent camps, and camping grounds. During the day the tourists go out in buses and photograph the lions, and the gazelles, and the herds of elephants. They photograph the Masai, who oblige by posing for pictures but then request payment. Then they return to their luxury hotels for dinner and drinks and relax with the feeling that they are on a big-game safari.

Some of the hotels are built near watering holes, so the animals come directly to the tourists while the tourists have dinner or drink at the bar. The most famous of these is Treetops, a hotel built on stilts above a watering hole and salt lick in the Nyandarua Mountains. Every evening a herd of elephants, along with zebras, gazelles, and baboons, shows up. The baboons at Treetops have become familiar with the tourists but have a reputation for sneaking into open windows and stealing cameras and other objects.

Treetops was made famous when, in 1952, Princess Elizabeth of England was staying there and heard the news that her father had died and that she had become queen.

At the Samburu lodge tourists relax in the evenings by watching crocodiles eating raw meat that the hotel staff leaves by the banks of the river that flows past the hotel.

Other tourists come for Kenya's beaches and to relax among the coconut palms, to eat mangos, or to snorkel around Kenya's coral reef. Still others choose the old-style safari route, making the difficult trek to Lake Turkana or to Marsabit.

Over 400,000 tourists came to Kenya in 1986, and for the first time in Kenya's history tourism surpassed coffee as the country's largest income earner. The tourists spend their money in hotels and restaurants, buy safari suits, Kamba wood carvings, Masai spears made especially for them, and fashionable African jewelry.

Some 40,000 Kenyans are employed in the tourism industry—just slightly less than are employed in the entire manufacturing sector. Utali (Swahili for "tourism") College turns out graduates who will work as waiters, tour guides, hotel managers, and travel agents.

But critics of the tourism industry point out that it may be doing more harm than good. While tourists spend their money in Kenya, the government must also spend money to import the things the tourists want, such as European foods and alcoholic drinks.

Some Kenyans are worried about the influence of the foreigners. And indeed, many foreigners show little regard for African values—by, for example, swimming nude at the beaches, or by invading peoples' privacy by photographing them without permission. The influence of the tourists on young Kenyans is also a concern. Many young boys have learned to survive by hustling tourists for money. Kenyans also find it distasteful that their country has become a playground for wealthy European, American, and Japanese visitors.

And Kenya may not always be able to count on the tourist industry to earn money. Today Kenya is a "hot spot," but that could change at any time. A war or a coup could put an instant end to the tourist trade and destroy the investments that have been made in hotels and restaurants. Stories from Africa about the deadly disease AIDS (Acquired Immune Deficiency Syndrome) have already shaken the tourist industry; and though the Kenyan government has accused the foreign press of exaggerating the problem in Kenya, it has also cooperated with international health officials in efforts to battle this epidemic. So far the largest concentration of AIDS cases is farther west, in central Africa.

But the largest threat to the tourist industry is the threat to the animals themselves.

Endangering the Species

The elephant is the largest land mammal and one of the most intelligent animals on earth. Those who have observed elephants report that they stay in close-knit families and that each is very much an individual with its own personality. Left alone an elephant can live for sixty years.

But man has not been able to leave the elephant alone. In 1979 1.3 million elephants roamed freely in Africa. Today there are less than 700,000 remaining, and some experts predict that unless something is done, the herds will be halved again in five years' time. Despite the fact that Kenya banned hunting in 1976, elephants continue to be slaughtered for their ivory tusks.

Ivory fetches $150 a pound on the market, so one large tusk can be worth $5,000. Meanwhile most Kenyans earn less than $350 over an entire year. The ivory is shipped to Hong Kong, where it is carved or

Elephant tusks and a skull that were taken from poachers. Kenya's rangers have orders to shoot poachers on sight, but even some of the rangers have not been able to resist the lure of fast profits to be made from selling elephant ivory. Lindblad / African Wildlife Foundation

The rhinoceros is becoming an increasingly rare sight in Kenya, as poachers have slaughtered them for their horns, which are ground into powder and sold as aphrodisiacs in the Far East. Lindblad / African Wildlife Foundation

used for billiard balls, piano keys, and jewelry.

Likewise, rhinoceros horn can be sold for $200 a pound. Most of that ends up in Yemen, where the horns are made into dagger handles. Some rhino horn is shipped to Asia, where it is ground into a powder and used as a aphrodisiac, though there is no scientific evidence to suggest that it does anything at all. The one effect it has had, however, is that it has driven the rhino to the edge of extinction.

Poachers find that the possible gains from killing elephants and rhinos outweigh the risks. One of those risks is that they will themselves be killed. The Kenyan government has permitted rangers to shoot the poachers on sight if they are caught red-handed, but the vastness of the area that the rangers must cover makes it difficult for them to ever find the poachers. They are more likely to come across the remains of dead elephants with their tusks removed.

One of the most disturbing aspects of the poaching is that much of it has been done by the park rangers who have been hired to protect the animals. In early 1988 a scandal broke in Kenya that led to the firing of twenty-seven members of the Ministry of Tourism and Wildlife, some of whom were implicated in the selling of banned animal trophies. Members of some of Kenya's most powerful families have been accused of participating in this destructive trade.

The Cape buffalo is the animal considered to be the most dangerous to humans. Because of their poor eyesight, they have a tendency to charge at any creature they smell in the vicinity. Lindblad / African Wildlife Foundation

It is also expensive for a poor African country to protect the parks, especially when so many people in the country are in desperate need of assistance. Organizations such as the African Wildlife Foundation, based in Washington, D.C., have contributed to efforts to protect Kenya's wildlife, and there have been some positive results. The leopard, for example, which until recently was on the verge of extinction, is now in less danger.

The wildlife is not just an African concern but is the responsibility of all the world's people and governments.

In the last ten years, Kenya's elephant population has been reduced by half, to fewer than 700,000, due to poaching and to the conversion of the elephant's natural habitat into farmland. Many conservationists fear that in the near future the only remaining elephants will be in zoos. Lindblad / African Wildlife Foundation

Man Versus Beast: The Battle for Land

The Meru game park to the north of Mount Kenya is home to hundreds of elephants. After the rains the park is lush and green, and the elephants happily eat the grass and tree bark. But as the season wears on and the grass disappears, they go off looking for some high, wet ground in the forests around Mount Kenya.

Though the Meru reserve and the Mount Kenya forest are both preserves for the animals, the land between them had been given to landless farmers after independence. Where once the elephants' path to the high ground was through deserted wilderness, it now takes them through farmers' fields.

An elephant can eat 300 pounds of forage a day. A herd of elephants passing through an area can trample or eat everything in sight.

The Kenyan government has a program for reimbursing farmers for the damage caused by elephants, but as the population expands and new land is cultivated more and more farmland is destroyed, and the government hasn't been able to keep up. Kenya's rapidly expanding population and increasing demand for farmland are destined to pit human needs against those of Kenya's wildlife.

The expanding farms also have an indirect effect on the animals. Though there are no farmers in Masai Mara, settlers around the park have put up fences. Even though the fences are not in the reserves, they have prevented the animals from migrating and seeking pasture and water.

For the Kenyan government the challenge is to find the balance between the needs of the human population and those of the wildlife. For Europeans coming to Kenya the animals are a delight to behold. But the African farmer whose crops are destroyed by elephants and whose cattle are eaten by lions thinks, understandably, that they are a nuisance.

Nairobi National Park is only a few minutes from the center of the city. Jason Lauré

Many Kenyans feel that they are paying too high a price to preserve the animals so the rest of the world can come and enjoy them. If the wildlife is part of the heritage of humankind, they say, then it is everyone's responsibility to pay the price. But Kenyans need both the farmland and the wildlife to earn money.

Every day, as the answers to this dilemma become more difficult to find and the country's problems become more pressing, the future of Africa's wildlife looks increasingly bleak.

Looking to the Future

Africa is a continent in crisis. Nineteen of the twenty-five poorest countries in the world are African. From Ethiopia and the countries of the West African Sahel—the dry strip of countries just south of the the Sahara Desert—horrible images of famine and death have accompanied cries for help flashing urgently across the world. Many of these countries still face years of food shortages and uncertainty. In southern Africa, wars in Angola and Mozambique have led to mass starvation, deaths, and hundreds of thousands of refugees. In South Africa 24 million Africans still live under an oppressive apartheid system that is harsher than what Kenyans endured under colonialism.

A Samburu girl in front of her hut.   Amy Zuckerman

Kenya's neighbor Uganda, a beautiful and fertile land with an old and rich culture, has been victimized by two brutal dictators, Idi Amin and Milton Obote, who between them have butchered hundreds of thousands of Ugandans.

In comparison, Kenya has been fortunate. Tribalism, while an obstacle to nationalism, has rarely turned into violence as it did in Burundi, where 200,000 members of one ethnic group were slaughtered in 1972. Kenya has suffered famines in its northern regions, but nothing as severe as in Ethiopia. Corruption and abuses of political power have been common in Kenya, but have not led to the overthrow of the government as in Nigeria, Uganda, Ghana, and other African countries.

Only one of Kenya's three newspapers is controlled by the government. In contrast, many African countries do not allow private newspapers to exist at all. Still, Kenya cannot be said to have a free press. Editors engage in self-censorship. They know not to print criticism of the government, or of people who are close to the president, if they want to keep their jobs.

Kenyans are allowed to vote, but only for the candidates of the ruling party, and they are allowed to speak freely so long as they don't criticize the government. Many of those who have opposed the government have been arrested for sedition and held in detention for years without trials.

But the dreams that accompanied *uhuru* still live on in Kenya. Though Kenyans realize that their quality of life is relatively good, their hopes and aspirations cannot be satisfied by the knowledge that they are better off than others in Africa. Kenyans continue to struggle to build the nation that they want for themselves.

Wabenzi and *Wananchi*

Kenya today is a country of rich and poor, *wabenzi* and *wananchi*. A

Mercedes-Benz can cost $150,000 in Kenya, and many people don't think twice about buying one—or two. Meanwhile the people they hire to wash their new cars, or to keep their lawns trim or to guard their homes, make only $30 per month. The average Kenyan earns less than $350 per year, while some 500 Kenyans are millionaires, many of them keeping their money in foreign banks.

The resentment that the poor feel toward the rich is evident. The rich need high walls and guards around their homes. It is not safe to walk on the streets of Nairobi at night as gangs of youths prowl, looking for victims. Groups called *panga* gangs, after the machetes they carry, commonly attack people in their homes or cars. They are angry, violent, and usually educated, which adds to their frustration at not being able to find work.

Kenya's newspapers are full of stories of grisly murders and robberies, but the Kenyan authorities are doing all that they can to prevent such tales from leaking out of the country and frightening off the tourists.

The Issue That Won't Go Away

The land issue that dominated Kenya's history seems destined to dominate its future. That issue looms even larger in light of one chilling fact: Kenya has the world's highest rate of population growth. The 22 million people in Kenya today are increasing their numbers by a compounded rate of over 4 percent per year.

At this growth rate Kenya's population will reach almost 40 million by the year 2000. And one third or more of that population could be without land. Today more than half of Kenya's population is under the age of fifteen, and it is their future that is so much in doubt.

These people will truly be the dispossessed. Without land they will

have no roots, no links with the past, nothing to fall back on. The land issue threatens Kenya's political stability as well as its ability to feed itself.

The streets of Nairobi today are visibly more crowded than they were five years ago. More beggars can be found staking out a piece of sidewalk from which to plead for money. Urbanization, already rapidly increasing, is bound to cause more problems. More than a million people now live in Nairobi, and by the turn of the century the city could be home to 5 million people, many of them unemployed.

Even for a person who finds a job in the city—a job like being a clerk or working in a store, or as a doorman at a hotel—life is difficult. Wages are at levels that allow people little more than the bare necessities. At lunchtime Kenya's work force eats along roadsides or in the parks. Lunch may consist of a bag of French fries and a Coke, or half a loaf of bread and some tea. It is inexpensive and filling fare to get them through the long afternoons, but not the kind of diet that produces happy, productive workers.

Along with the unemployed there are the underemployed, people with very low-paying, part-time work that is below subsistence levels.

Industry

One of the challenges that Kenya faces in the future is providing more and better jobs for the urban workers and providing jobs in the towns to keep people out of the cities. Today only 8 percent of Kenya's labor force is employed by industry. Yet Kenya is the most industrialized country in East Africa.

Because goods are scarce, Kenyans throw away almost nothing. Virtually all scrap metal is reused in some manner. Here a man makes kerosene lanterns out of old oil cans.
UNEP / Asman Kasoro

Most of Kenya's industry is small-scale. The largest enterprise in the country is the brewery, and beer is the most frequently purchased item in the country. Recently Kenya Breweries began exporting its award-winning Tusker Premium to the United States, but many more export industries will be needed to supply a significant number of jobs to the urban poor.

This label is designed for Kenya's Tusker beer, one of the nation's most important companies. Increasing exports of Kenyan beer are bringing much-needed foreign exchange.
Kenya Brewing Company

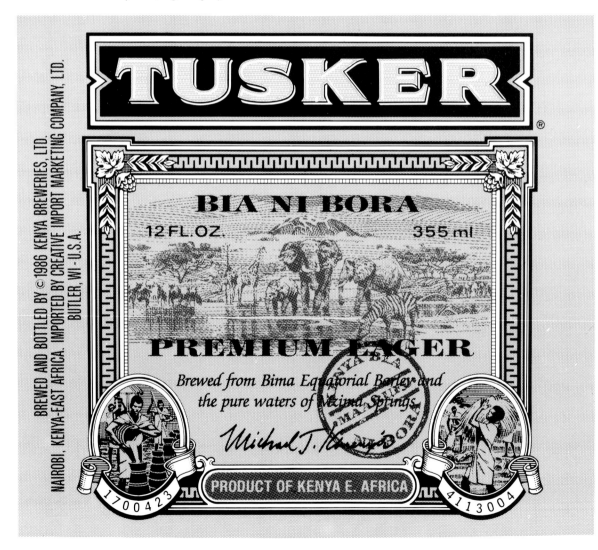

Other goods bought within the country—such as soaps, cooking oils, and cigarettes—have allowed the development of successful businesses. But for these businesses to expand and prosper, Kenya needs to reach out to export markets.

The natural markets are neighbors Uganda and Tanzania. For several years the three countries tried to open their borders for each others' goods. They formed the East African Community and shared the costs of a regional airline, railroads, mail, and telecommunications. The plan made sense, because these institutions had been shared by the three countries under colonialism. But politics in the independent countries got in the way, and the East African Community collapsed in 1976.

The borders were closed. Some Kenyan goods were smuggled into Tanzania, but the volume of business was not large enough to be of benefit to Kenya's industries.

Recently the borders between Kenya and its neighbors were once again opened, and there have been some attempts at increasing economic cooperation among the three countries. But one of the old problems still exists: Kenya is much more economically developed than its neighbors. Tanzanians and Ugandans crave Kenya's manufactured goods. And they want the Kenya shilling, which would allow them to buy imported goods such as stereos, cameras, cars, and clothes, which are available in Nairobi but not in Kampala or Dar es Salaam.

The Ugandan and Tanzanian governments feel that Kenya is the only country that benefits from the open borders. The Tanzanians have also complained that tourists cross the border to see animals in the Serengeti, but pass the night (and spend their money) in Kenya.

Though there are still disputes, the three countries know that they must cooperate if they are to industrialize.

Another reason that industrialization has not succeeded is that Kenya and many other African nations have not been able to break free of the

A Somali shop owner, on the left, sits with one of his customers, a Turkana man, at Loiyangalini on the eastern shore of Lake Turkana. Many of the merchants in northern Kenya are Somalis.   Amy Zuckerman

economies they inherited from the colonial powers. The colonial economy was designed to serve the European colonial power. A colony such as Kenya was expected to export raw materials to Britain and to do business with British companies by importing manufactured goods.

The African colonies did not trade among themselves. Rail lines and roads led from areas of production to ports for export. The colonial powers encouraged the colonies to be dependent, and Kenya today remains very much dependent on the West to buy Kenyan coffee and tea and as the source for imported manufactured goods.

Even when Kenya produces a product, it must import the parts. For example, a car called the Uhuru is built in Kenya from Toyota parts imported from Japan. The assembly plant provides employment for some Kenyan workers but not nearly as many as if the car were built from the ground up. Those jobs are still in Japan. In addition, the market for the car is limited in Kenya, and it is not likely to expand into a large industry.

Recently, some oil has been discovered in Kenya's northern drylands, but no one is sure if there is enough under the ground to justify the costs of pumping it out. Oil companies have been exploring in Kenya since 1950, and Kenyans have long hoped that oil would save the economy. Kenya's experts have warned against too much optimism.

Coffee

Though tourism surpassed coffee production as the number-one foreign exchange earner in 1986, coffee is the mainstay of the economy, employing thousands of small farmers and giving them a cash income that in turn supports Kenya's small manufacturing sector.

The price that Kenya's farmers receive for their coffee depends on factors that are beyond Kenya's control. When, for example, a frost killed much of Brazil's coffee in 1975 and 1976, the shortage caused the world price to go up. And when Kenya's coffee farmers had more money, the entire country prospered. Skyscrapers rose in Nairobi. People bought consumer products, and there were jobs available in the factories.

But when Brazil's crop was back to normal in 1978, coffee prices fell, and Kenya went into debt. The same cycle was repeated in 1986 and 1987. Likewise, tea prices are dependent on factors beyond Kenya's control. And since all the coffee and tea are purchased by Western countries, Kenya finds itself very much dependent on outside powers.

Kenya's Foreign Trade

Trade figures for countries that rely on exporting crops and other natural resources change frequently as world prices shift, and it is often misleading to apply the standards of measurement we use in the United States to the economy of a developing nation. These figures are designed to give a portrait of the *general trends* of Kenya's economy; the specific percentages change each year.

Kenya's Leading Imports

Crude oil	33.3%
Motor vehicles & parts	27.0%
Machinery	12.8%
Glass	4.5%
Vegetable oils	2.5%
Chemicals	2.2%
Wire products	2.1%
Other imports, each at less than 2.1%	15.6%

The percentages represent share of dollars earned from total imports.

Coffee and tea account for the major share of Kenya's yearly export earnings.

A similar situation, left over from colonial days, exists in most African countries, where the modern economy is based on the export of a

Kenya's Leading Exports

Coffee	26.5%
Refined petroleum products	26.0%
Tea	14.2%
Cement	3.6%
Sisal	2.0%
Other exports, each at less than 2.0%	27.7%

The percentages represent share of dollars earned from total exports.

Kenya produces no oil of its own, but imports crude oil to a refinery in Mombasa and then exports refined products to Uganda, Rwanda, Burundi, Zaire, and Sudan. Cement is also exported to these neighboring countries.

Most of Kenya's exports go to the United Kingdom (12.7%), West Germany (11%), Uganda (10.1%), the United States (6.1%), and the Netherlands (5.1%).

In 1987 Kenya spent $651 million more on imports than it earned from its exports. This is called a trade deficit.

Kenya's major sources for imports are the United Kingdom (15.1%), Saudi Arabia (14.9%), West Germany (8.4%), Japan (7.8%), France (3.1%), and the Netherlands (2.6%).

single crop or mineral. Uganda also exports coffee, Ghana exports cocoa, Zambia produces copper, Senegal produces peanuts, etc.

The problem with exporting only one or two items is that if the price for that one item falls, the entire country suffers. In the United States, which has a diversified economy, if prices for farm products are low, jobs can be found in manufacturing. In Kenya if the price of coffee falls, there is nothing to fall back on. Today the prices for most of Africa's exports are low.

Kenya has been criticized for using its best land to grow coffee for export while sometimes not having enough food to feed its people. Realizing that this will cause serious problems in the future, the government has been encouraging farmers to grow more food. They have had some success, and Kenya has avoided serious famines—though there have been times of critical food shortages, especially in the dry northern areas.

Despite its attempts to industrialize, Kenya is essentially an agricultural country. The future is in the land.

The Threatening Sands

Driving along the dirt roads in Kenya's northern districts one often sees large burlap bags by the roadsides. In the bags is charcoal, blackened wood that has been smoldered under sand and turned into this fuel. The large blackened bags will be loaded onto trucks and transported to Nairobi or other towns, where people will burn it in small metal stoves to cook their meals.

In the bush along the roads smoke rises from the pits where more trees are being burned into charcoal.

Kenya is in desperate need of fuel. When oil prices rose drastically in the early 1970s, it greatly damaged Kenya's fragile economy, and the demand for cheap fuel like charcoal increased. But the cutting down of trees has devastated the country's sensitive ecology, and the costs of the charcoal are higher than most people realize.

Without trees to hold down the soil, erosion has taken place and

A woman in western Kenya carrying water in an earthenware jug. Many women in rural areas haul water for several miles every day.   The Hutchison Library

fertile topsoil has disappeared. In a matter of years savanna has turned to desert, and potentially productive farmland has disappeared. With the population so concentrated in the fertile highlands, Kenya needs these marginal lands to be productive.

It is not only in the savanna where there has been ecological damage. The dense forests that once surrounded Mount Kenya and other highland areas has been reduced to slim strips of trees. The wood has been used for fuel and for construction, but little of it has been replaced.

Barren, windy hillsides lie where forests once stood. When it rains, the topsoils run off the land and the water carves deep ruts in the earth.

And the damage continues.

More than 80 percent of Kenya's population is still involved in agriculture of one sort or another, and this is likely to remain the center of economic activity for the foreseeable future. People will have to begin to farm the lower, drier savanna, but they will also have to take care not to damage the environment. Kenya is now trying to teach people how to build more efficient ovens to save fuel. Rural farmers are being encouraged to plant trees and to terrace their farms to reduce soil erosion.

But for now the land is being destroyed faster than it is being reclaimed.

Kenya and the World

African countries have attempted to cooperate among themselves to reduce dependence on the wealthy countries of the West. The idea that a united Africa would be stronger than 52 separate countries is called Pan-Africanism. During the early 1960s, as African countries were becoming independent, an organization was set up to work toward this goal. It was called the Organization of African Unity, or the OAU.

But political differences among African countries have prevented the OAU from achieving many of its goals. As with the United Nations, it is often difficult to get individual countries to reach agreements. The OAU continues to meet to discuss issues of common concern, but African unity is still a distant prospect.

Within the East African region, Kenya early on found itself at odds with its neighbors. Both Uganda, under President Milton Obote, and Tanzania, under Julius Nyerere, chose socialist paths of development,

A man piles charcoal into tins for sale. In order to earn money, some Kenyans have leveled acres of Kenya's scarce woodlands, set the trees afire, and covered them with sand. The wood continues to smoulder under the sand and eventually becomes charcoal. It is then sold in the towns, where people use it for cooking. The government, with the help of international organizations, is looking for inexpensive alternatives for cooking fuel in order to help save Kenya's forests. Michael Maren

and Kenyatta's capitalist orientation put strains on the relationship among the three.

Kenya suspected that Obote had been encouraging dissent among the Luo in western Kenya, so the 1971 military coup that replaced Obote with Idi Amin was welcomed in Nairobi. But Amin quickly became an international embarrassment, and Kenya distanced itself from the dictator.

To the north, relations with Somalia, which had been tense since the guerrilla war over Kenya's Northeast Province in 1963, took a turn for the better in early 1988 when Somalia, for the first time, renounced its claim to the land. The conflict with Somalia had given Kenya common cause with Ethiopia, which had similarly been threatened by Somali designs for "Greater Somalia." Despite Ethiopia's radical Marxist orientation, Kenya and Ethiopia remained closely allied in the face of a common enemy.

Kenyatta followed a course of noninterference in other countries' external affairs. He issued very little criticism of Amin and stayed away from most international political issues in his day. His focus was squarely on what he thought best for Kenya. (It has been suggested that one of the reasons for Kenyatta's staying out of international politics was his dislike of flying.)

Though Kenya maintained cordial relations with the Soviet Union and publicly charted a course of nonalignment, Kenyatta led Kenya firmly into the Western camp. Britain still maintains a military presence in Kenya, and the United States has secured military landing rights there in the event of a conflict in the region.

In 1976, when Arab hijackers forced an Air France jet to land at Kampala's Entebbe Airport in Uganda, Kenya allowed the Israeli strike force that rescued the hostages to land and refuel in Nairobi. Despite the fact that Kenya and Israel do not have official relations, the two countries are close. Israeli companies have built many of Kenya's roads and buildings, and the two countries cooperate on security matters.

Under President Moi, Kenya has closely followed in Kenyatta's footsteps. Relations with the United States remain strong, though some tension developed after Kenya was charged with violating human rights in 1986 and 1987. Still, the United States considers Kenya to be its best friend in black Africa.

U.S. foreign aid to Kenya is an important element in the Kenyan economy and Kenya is the largest recipient of American aid in sub-Saharan Africa. This aid relationship goes back to even before Kenya's independence. In 1962 and 1963, a famine struck East Africa, and even Kenya's fertile highlands suffered from food shortages. President John F. Kennedy sent tons of American corn to relieve the shortages. Kenyans, who are more accustomed to large, white maize, found the American corn very strange. They were, however, extremely appreciative of the American efforts, and Kenyans will often proudly recount to American visitors the story of how President Kennedy helped them when they were in need.

Kenya is trying its best to attract more American companies to invest there and help provide jobs for the future. So far, however, foreign companies have invested relatively little in Kenya—though 120 American companies are represented in Nairobi.

Kenya still maintains a very special relationship with the United Kingdom. The United Kingdom is still Kenya's largest trading partner, and the two countries remain closely tied politically despite some differences over the years.

Kenya's elite still aspire to send their children to Britain for an education—though the United States is becoming an equally popular destination—and the influence of the British legal and political systems keeps the two countries in close affinity.

Kenya is a member of the British Commonwealth, an organization of former British colonies that includes Canada, Australia, Zimbabwe, Malaysia and others. The leaders of the commonwealth countries meet every year to discuss matters of political and economic interest. Athletes from the member states compete regularly in the Commonwealth Games, and regular cultural exchanges are promoted.

The purpose of the Commonwealth is to enhance economic, political, and cultural links between Britain and her former colonies, and among the several states. The member states receive economic advantages such as reduced trade and travel restrictions.

President Moi has taken more of an international outlook than Kenyatta and has sought to become a regional leader by offering to mediate disputes between other African countries.

Looking Ahead

Domestic matters must still be Kenya's main area of concern, and the issues haven't changed all that much since colonial times. For Kenya's leaders there are no easy answers and not much time. Kenya's people are still waiting for the promises of independence to be fulfilled.

Political tensions are certain to increase along with pressure on land resources. The population has so far been patient, but students and others are beginning to agitate for jobs, for more democracy, and for an economic system that they believe would bring more resources to the common people.

These are crucial times for Kenya. The urgent economic and population pressures make it more difficult for the country to slowly find its balance between the modern and the traditional and between demands for land and the need to preserve the environment. In this land of jet planes and computers people want solutions quickly. And in this land of strong traditions and fierce ethnic pride, rivalries continue to disrupt the society and make rapid agreements more difficult to reach.

Despite the problems and crises Kenya has endured, the spirit of *Harambee* persists. Kenyans are optimistic that they will be able to work out their disagreements and overcome the challenges facing their young nation.

Evening

The dusk doesn't last very long on the equator. As the sun sinks toward the horizon it seems to accelerate, and day turns quickly to night.

In the villages, the chickens scurry back into their coops. Those that don't make it back will fall victim to the fox and the mongoose, which prowl around in the night. Goats are tethered, and issue shrill cries of protest at losing their freedom for the night. The cows are penned in.

By the light of kerosene lanterns, families cluster around dinner tables to enjoy *ugali*, maize and beans. The sounds of crickets pierce the cool night air.

In Nairobi the shops are closed. The last of the evening rush-hour traffic leaves the streets deserted. People gather in restaurants for a few bottles of Tusker. Goat meat is roasted over a large open fire. The night clubs will open later.

The night watchmen take over the sidewalks. They light fires in trash bins outside the shops they will guard for the night. Beggars gather to count the change they have earned today.

In the desert the sun sifts through a dusty haze, giving the harsh stony landscape a soft, red glow. Over Lake Turkana, a few El Molo fishermen fold their nets and watch one of the most magnificent sunsets on earth: The sky is deep violet and crimson.

The minibuses full of tourists return to the game lodges, where dinner is waiting. Crocodiles that had been sunning on riverbanks slide back into the water. The air vibrates with the force of flapping wings.

From Nairobi the night train heads for the coast. A dhow returns to Lamu island and is tied to a buoy offshore. The young men fold the sail and dive into the Indian Ocean to swim the last few yards home.

In Mombasa, the call for the evening prayer echoes in the silenced city.

Bibliography

General

Lamb, David. *The Africans.* New York: Random House, 1982.
  Good general book on Africa, full of anecdotes.
Trillo, Richard. *The Rough Guide to Kenya.* New York: Routledge & Kegan Paul,
  1987.
  The best tourist guide to Kenya available.
Ungar, Sanford J. *Africa: The People and Politics of an Emerging Continent.* New York:
  Simon and Schuster, 1985.
  The best general book on Africa. Recommended for the general reader to get a
  feeling for the people and problems of continent.

Chapter II: The Land

Kaplan, Irving, with Margarita K. Dobert [et al.]. *Area Handbook for Kenya.* Washing-
  ton: U.S. Government Printing Office, 1985.
  Statistics and facts about Kenya. An excellent reference.
Rosenblum, Mort, and Doug Williamson. *Squandering Eden: Africa at the Edge.* New
  York: Harcourt Brace Jovanovich, 1987.
  An American journalist's impressions of the decay and destruction of Africa.

Chapter III: The Peoples

Kenyatta, Jomo. *Facing Mount Kenya.* New York: Vintage, 1965.
  The book on the Kikuyu.
———. *My People of Kikuyu* and *The Life of Chief Wangombe.* Nairobi: Oxford
  University Press, 1966.
  Kenyatta remembers. A rare look at Kikuyu life in precolonial Kenya.

Chapter IV: Early History

Davidson, Basil. *Africa in History.* New York: Macmillan, 1968.
>Good general history encompassing the entire continent. Davidson is one of the first Western historians to take African history seriously.

Gould, Stephen Jay. *The Mismeasure of Man.* New York: W.W. Norton & Company, 1981.
>Fascinating exposé on misguided attempts by scientists to prove that black and other nonwhite races are inferior.

Harris, Joseph E. *Africans and Their History.* New York: Mentor, 1972; revised edition, 1987.
>Useful general history of Africa. Good complement to Davidson's book.

Ingham, Kenneth. *A History of East Africa.* New York: Praeger, 1962.
>Detailed history concentrating on the East African coast. Out of print.

Miller, Charles. *The Lunatic Express: An Entertainment in Imperialism.* New York: Ballantine Books, 1971.
>A highly entertaining tale of the building of the railway from Mombasa. It also includes a wealth of details about the early arrival of the British in Kenya.

Moorehead, Alan. *The White Nile.* New York: Harper & Brothers, 1960.
>The classic book about the men who set off into Africa to find the source of the Nile. It should be read after its companion book, *The Blue Nile.*

Chapter V: Colonialism and Independence

Dinesen, Isak. *Out of Africa.* New York: Vintage, 1972. First published, 1937.
>Danish writer's autobiographical book about her years as coffee farmer outside of Nairobi.

Itote, Waruhiu, *Mau Mau General.* Nairobi: East African Publishing House, 1967.
>The real story of the Mau Mau told from the inside.

Kenyatta, Jomo. *Suffering Without Bitterness.* Nairobi: East African Publishing House, 1968.
>A collection of Kenyatta's speeches before and after independence.

Meredith, Martin. *The First Dance of Freedom: Black Africa in the Post-War Era.* New York: Harper & Row, 1984.
>One of the best books written about the coming of independence to Africa.

Murray-Brown, Jeremy. *Kenyatta.* Winchester, MA: Allen & Unwin, 1972.
>The definitive biography of Kenyatta.

Ngugi wa Thiong'o. *The River Between.* London: Heinemann, 1965.
>Novel about the changes wrought by the arrival of missionaries in a Kikuyu village.

Rosberg, Carl and John Nottingham. *The Myth of "Mau Mau": Nationalism in Kenya.* New York: Meridian, 1966.
  Academic history of the growing nationalist movement in Kenya from the 1920s. The first work to portray Mau Mau as an organized land revolt rather than a series of violent acts committed at random.

Chapter VI: The Fruits of Independence

Attwood, William. *The Reds and the Blacks, a Personal Adventure.* New York: Harper & Row, 1967.
  An American diplomat looks at the early days of independence in Kenya and Guinea.
Karimi, Joseph, and Philip Ochieng. *The Kenyatta Succession.* Nairobi: Transafrica, 1980.
  Revelations of the plots and machinations surrounding Kenyatta's death, by two of Kenya's leading journalists. Also serves as a text on the wheeling and dealing that drives politics in Kenya.
Ngugi wa Thiong'o. *Petals of Blood.* London: Heinemann, 1977.
  Novel about neocolonialism and the selling out of Kenya.

Chapter VII: An Education

Mwangi, Meja. *Kill Me Quick.* London: Heinemann, 1973.
  Interesting first novel by a Kenyan writer who knows the underside of life in urban Kenya.

Chapter VIII: Arts and Culture

Mugo, Micere Githae, and Ngugi Wa Thiong'o. *The Trial of Dedan Kimathi.* London: Heinemann Educational Books, 1976.
  Good example of the use of drama with a political message for the people of Kenya.
Ngugi wa Thiong'o. *Decolonizing the Mind: The Politics of Language in African Literature.* London: James Currey, Heinemann, 1986.
  Ngugi argues for the use of African languages by African writers and discusses the negative impact of the West on African literature and culture.
Turnbull, Colin. *The Lonely African.* New York: Simon and Schuster, 1962.
  An anthropologist discusses the impact of the West on traditional cultures.
———. *Tradition and Change in African Tribal Life.* Cleveland: World Pub. Co., 1966.
  A similar book for the younger reader.

Chapter IX: Safari

Caras, Roger. *Mara Simba: The African Lion.* New York: Holt, Reinhart and Winston, 1985.
   Follows the life of a single lion in Kenya's Masai Mara reserve.
Moss, Cynthia. *Elephant Memories: Thirteen Years in the Life of an Elephant Family.* New York: William Morrow & Company, 1988.
————. *Portraits in the Wild.* London: Hamish Hamilton, 1976.
   Both of Moss's books are musts for animal lovers.

Chapter X: Looking to the Future

Ngugi wa Thiong'o. *Detained: A Writer's Prison Diary.* Nairobi: Heinemann, 1981.
   Ngugi's thoughts about politics in Kenya and elsewhere, originally written on toilet paper while he was detained by Kenyatta's government.
Whitaker, Jennifer Seymour. *How Can Africa Survive?* New York: Harper & Row, 1988.
   A realistic inventory of Africa's seemingly insoluble problems.

Filmography

The government of Kenya has gone out of its way to encourage film producers to come and film there. Film companies often employ hundreds of extras and pump millions of dollars into the local economy. Many of the films shot there are actually about Kenya, while others simply use the scenery. *Quest for Fire*, a film about early man, was filmed in part in Kenya. Kenyans sometimes like to refer to Nairobi as "the Hollywood of Africa."

The following is a selected list of films about Kenya.

Born Free. Columbia, 1965.
  The story of Joy and George Adamson and their relationship with Elsa the lioness, based on the true story of their work in Kenya's Meru reserve.

Out of Africa. MCA Universal, 1985.
  Film based on Isak Dinesen's book of the same name shows breathtaking scenes of Kenya and contains interesting bits of colonial history.

White Mischief. Columbia, 1988.
  From James Fox's book of the same name, explores the mystery surrounding the murder of Lord Errol in colonial Kenya of the 1920's. Captures the decadence of "Happy Valley."

The Kitchen Toto. Cannon Films, 1988.
  The Kitchen Toto (Kitchen Boy) is a young Kikuyu whose father has been murdered by Mau Mau fighters. To support the family he goes to work for a white policeman. Shows the dilemma that many Kenyans faced during the Mau Mau uprising.

Sheena. Columbia, 1985.
  Exceptionally foolish film, shot entirely in Kenya, full of every misleading cliché about Africa ever filmed.

The Flame Trees of Thika.
Made-for-TV movie from the book by Elspeth Huxley recounts her childhood on a coffee farm in Kenya.

Year of the Wildebeest.
Exceptional among the hundreds of nature films shot in Kenya. Follows the herds of wildebeest on their migration through East Africa.

Discography

Kenyan Music Available in the United States

Recordings from Kenya can be found in many large record stores. These are a sampling of interesting discs in a number of styles.

Traditional

Africa: Ceremonial and Folk Music
  Nonesuch H-72063
Africa: Witchcraft and Ritual Music
  Nonesuch H-72066

Folk

African Rhythms; Songs From Kenya Sung by D. Nzomo
  Asch Records AH 8503
The Nairobi Sound; Acoustic and Electric Guitar Music of Kenya
  Original Music OMA 101

Pop

Original. Simba Wanyika Orchestra.
  African Music Gallery AMG 003
Benga Beat. Shirati Jazz.
  World Circuit WCB 003
Ukumbushu. Mbaraka Mwinsheshe.
  Polydor Nigeria Polp 550

Index

References to illustrations are in *italics*.

Kenya, Mount, 22–23, *23*, 24, 62,
   154
  Kikuyu homes at, *39*
Kenya, name, derivation of, 23, 24
Kenya Plan, The, 93
Kenya's People's Union (KPU), 105
Kenyatta, Jomo, 77–80, 83, 85,
   88–89, *92*, *93*, 94
  death of, 113
  Facing Mount Kenya, 40
  government of, 107–9
  Kisumu massacre and, 111–12
  as president, 96–97, 99–107,
   109–13, 172
  statue of, *98*
Kenyatta Conference Center, Nairobi,
   105
Kiembu language, 41
Kikuyu Central Association, 85, 86
Kikuyu people, 23, 24, 37–41, *39*, 62
  arrested after Mau Mau uprising, *91*
  and British settlers, 75–77
  and independence, 89–95, 99
  Kenyatta and, 88
  language of, 5, 41
  and Luo people, 43
  politics of, 95, 103, 107
  resistance to colonialism by, 84–95
Kilimanjaro (mountain), 24, 144
Kilindini, Mombasa, 15–16
Kill Me Quick (Mwangi), 125
Kilwa, 63, 64
Kimathi, Dedan, 97
Kimathi Street, Nairobi, *34*, 97
Kimeru language, 41
King's East African Rifles, 86
Kipsigis people, 49, *49*
Kisumu, 28, *76*
  massacre at, 111–12
kitchen Swahili, 67

Koran, study of, 2–3
KPU (Kenya's People's Union), 105
Krapf, Johann Ludwig, 24, 69
Kushite civilization, 61

lakes in Rift Valley, 27
Lamu, 16–17, 63
land ownership, 11–13, 28, 159–61
  African demands for, 85, 92
  and colonialism, 80–81
  women's rights to, 126–27
languages, 4–5, 24, 41, 132–33
  English, 4, 7, 120, 132–33
  Jalou, 43, 103
  Kalenjin, 49
  spoken in secondary schools, 122
  Swahili, 66–67
lanterns, from oil cans, *160*
Leakey, Louis, 60
Leakey, Mary, 60
Leakey, Phillip, *108*
Leakey, Richard, 22, 61
legends, 38–40, 60
Lenana (Masai chief), 75
leopards, 153
lions, 17, 144–46, *145*
literature
  as oral tradition, 131–33
  of protest, 133–34
Livingston, David, 69
Longonot, Mount, *26*
long rains, 14
Lucy (hominid fossil), 61
Luhya people, 42, 43, 103
Luo people, 3, *3*, 28, 42–43, 62
  and independence, 99
  and Kisumu massacre, 111–12
  language of (Jaluo), 5, 43, 103
  politics of, 95, 103